Teaching Social Science in Schools

Teaching Social Science in Schools

NCERT's New Textbook Initiative

ALEX M. GEORGE
AMMAN MADAN

⑤SAGE Los Angeles • London • New Delhi • Singapore • Washington DC
www.sagepublications.com

First published in 2009 by

SAGE Publications India Pvt Ltd
B 1/I-1 Mohan Cooperative Industrial Area
Mathura Road, New Delhi 110 044, India
www.sagepub.in

SAGE Publications Inc
2455 Teller Road
Thousand Oaks,
California 91320, USA

SAGE Publications Ltd
1 Oliver's Yard, 55 City Road
London EC1Y 1SP, United Kingdom

SAGE Publications Asia-Pacific Pte Ltd
33 Pekin Street
#02-01 Far East Square
Singapore 048763

Published by Vivek Mehra for SAGE Publications India Pvt Ltd, typeset in 10/12.5 pt Palatino by Star Compugraphics Private Limited, Delhi and printed at Chaman Enterprises, New Delhi.

Library of Congress Cataloging-in-Publication Data

George, Alex M., 1972–
    Teaching social science in schools: NCERT's new textbook initiative/Alex M. George, Amman Madan.
        p. cm.
    1. Social sciences—Study and teaching (Secondary)—India.   I. Madan, Amman, 1966–   II. Title.

| H62.5.I5G46 | 300.71'254—dc22 | 2009 | 2008048388 |

ISBN: 978-81-7829-904-4 (PB)

The SAGE Team: Ashok R. Chandran, Sushmita Banerjee, Amrita Saha and Trinankur Banerjee

To all the teachers who rose above bad textbooks,
poor facilities and oppressive school organizations,
and made a difference in the lives of young people.
May your tribe increase!

CONTENTS

List of Extracts from School Textbooks   ix

Preface   xi

Acknowledgements   xv

Chapter 1 Parents   1

Chapter 2 Teachers   31

Chapter 3 Students   59

Chapter 4 Educationists   65

About the Authors   92

LIST OF EXTRACTS FROM
SCHOOL TEXTBOOKS

1.1	Learning to Think	2
1.2	Broadening their Vision	2
1.3	Learning about the Real World	5
1.4	Eklavya Used Pictures to Teach	9
1.5	Local Contexts: Everyday Work in Kashmir	10
1.6	Local Contexts: The Proud Produce of Kashmir	11
1.7	E-mail from a Teacher	14
1.8	Discuss with Your Child	16
1.9	Questions that Connect to Reality	16
1.10	Learning to See Deeper Truths	19
1.11	Beyond Textbooks	22
1.12	The World Upside Down?	27
1.13	Or, Is this the World Upside Down?	28
2.1	Pictures to Ponder About	38
2.2	Depicting Concepts	39
2.3	Pictures to make you Wonder	40
2.4	Connecting Textbooks with Life	41
2.5	Making Sense of a Complex World	41
2.6	Framing the Noteworthy: Using Boxes	42
2.7	Highlighting Key Ideas	43
2.8	Practising and Consolidating the Grasp of a Basic Concept	46
2.9	Unforgettable Lessons	51
2.10	Doable Activities	53

3.1	Not Just for Laughs	63
3.2	Open-ended Questions Work Better	64
4.1	The Old Way	66
4.2	The New Way	67
4.3	Concrete Examples for Complex Processes	72
4.4	Kids See Things Differently	74
4.5	Bringing Lives of Ordinary People into the Classroom	75
4.6a	The Issue is Important, not the Details	77
4.6b	The Issue is Important, not the Details	78
4.6c	The Issue is Important, not the Details	79
4.7	New Topics Keep Getting Added	82
4.8	One of the Best Illustrations	85
4.9	Lok Jumbish Social Science Textbooks from Rajasthan	90

PREFACE

The social sciences are often seen as easy, probably because they deal with issues and processes that surround us all the time, and on which we have ideas and positions. They are about people—our wealth, our problems and our values. Yet, this apparent simplicity is deceptive. Teaching the complexities of human beings is not easy. The recently developed social science textbooks of the National Council of Educational Research and Training (NCERT) are perhaps the most ambitious effort of its kind in India. They seek to address the challenges faced by social science education in India.

Social sciences in Indian schools are in an unenviable position. On the one hand, they are expected to shoulder the bulk of the normative expectations from schooling. Thus they are supposed to teach everything—from a commitment to keeping the streets clean to the internalization of a pluralist vision of the nation. Yet, on the other hand, they are treated as stepsisters of science. Science is seen as a solid grounding for a lucrative career, while social sciences are considered soft, trivial and for the weak. It puts the social sciences at the centre of a struggle over the purpose and meaning of schooling—is schooling only about getting a job or is it for becoming a better person?

Indian educationists have always had a wide vision of the purpose of education. Most policy documents have emphasized a cultural role for the social sciences, over and above the mundaneness of vocational knowledge. Social sciences are, after all, the most practical, dealing with affairs that everybody participates in, and best learnt by doing rather than reading. There is a consensus about the fact that the decline of the social sciences can only spell danger for the quality of public life in our country.

Yet, the quality of social science textbooks and classroom teaching has not risen to expectations. Too often there has been the lament that social sciences are dull and uninspiring. The most common complaint is that they are meant only for rote learning. Perhaps the cruellest cut of all has been students saying that there is nothing to understand in them, and that the social sciences are only for cramming.

historical Consciousness

How did the most exciting and the most relevant of themes—human beings, their environment and their affairs—sink to the nadir? The commercialization of our society supplies only part of the answer because, after all, the best paying jobs today are in applied social science. Some other parts of the picture are provided by: (*a*) the poor quality of textbooks, (*b*) the virtual absence of teacher education and (*c*) an examination system which focuses on the lowest common feature of all schools, that is, knowledge that can be acquired by rote.

Social science textbooks have traditionally been styled as a simple narration of facts. The idea that textbooks must provide a format which invites the active participation of students, has rarely been put into practice. Instead, there has been a linear monologue, punctuated only to check whether or not students have dutifully accepted what was uttered. Whenever any suggestion was offered for incorporation into the syllabus, it was added to the corpus. Thus, nothing got removed and the textbook grew into an encyclopaedia bearing two lines about everything under the sun. This may have made school textbooks good reference texts for those preparing for the civil services examination, but it also had the effect of worsening the textbooks as platforms for active learning. The cluttering up of the text with details only led to greater emphasis on memorizing all of them, since the examination could (and did) ask any bit of trivia. There was no time to try and deal reflectively with all of them in the classroom.

Many educationists in and outside the NCERT understood this problem. The solution, however, proved elusive since it lay not only in the creation of better textbooks, but also in the creation of a matching pattern of examinations, as well as complementary teacher education. There was also the problem of finding teachers who themselves could (and would) go beyond passive learning. Education that emphasized the active learning of the child would be available only then.

To be sure, there were several exceptions. Individual teachers here and there rose above trying circumstances to heroically inspire their students. Some students, especially those with the right kind of family support, occasionally succeeded in finding meaning and joy, even in dense and turgid texts. But these were a tiny, miniscule proportion; the opportunities wasted were immense.

Yet, a composite, multi-pronged shift is not in the realm of the impossible. It was demonstrated, for instance, in the 1980s by the non-governmental organization (NGO) Eklavya, which produced social science textbooks for grades 6 to 8 that focused on encouraging thinking and understanding, rather than rote. Eklavya combined innovative textbooks with teacher training, and rounded it off by getting the Madhya Pradesh government's permission for a board examination that stayed away from questions which could be answered by unthinking or rote learning.

The State Councils for Educational Research and Training (SCERTs) of Kerala and Delhi, among others, took matters forward. And now, the NCERT has brought out a completely new generation of social science textbooks, unlike any which this national body brought out in the past. The NCERT today works with the Central Board of Secondary Education (CBSE) to transform the examination pattern too.

Teacher education, however, remains largely unattended to. With the NCERT's textbooks being used in more than 9,000 schools across the country, the sheer scale of the task is enormous. While some school chains—like the Kendriya Vidyalayas—do organize their own in-house teacher training, the majority of schools and teachers are largely thrown back on to their own resources. Not surprisingly, the majority of teachers may find the new textbooks enigmatic; they may even try to teach these books just as the older ones were taught.

It is in this context that our book was written. This book has several objectives. One of them is to assist those teaching social sciences from grades 6 to 10 in understanding the premises behind the new generation of textbooks. We have therefore tried to prepare a book which can help teachers make the transition from the older kind of textbooks and their examination pattern into a new and much more enjoyable world of teaching.

We are also acutely aware of the limitations of our book. This book cannot replace a wide and comprehensive teacher

COMPARISON—wealthy (respectively unmarginalized students vs. dalit/marginalized folx? efficacy of NCERT

globalized english medium student

comprehension/consciousness NOT synonymous

rich + literate, ACK weeds out, balanced? confounding factors

what is the better question

looking @ a subset of literate students (wealthy)

looking @ the creation of globalized children

islamophobic doctrines?

look up

education programme aimed at the specifics of each school discipline. But we are confident that until such a programme emerges, the present book will fulfil a certain need.

It is not just the social science teacher who finds the NCERT's new textbooks radically different. Parents and children too are curious about these strangely colourful pages, their side remarks and their provocative questions. We have written for them too, knowing that their appreciation of the strategies and purposes of the textbooks is crucial. They may find our book helpful in getting much more out of their experience with the new textbooks.

deeply pro NCERT/ working w/ NCERT

The style of our book has been chosen keeping our readership in mind. It is designed so that the reader can dip in here and browse through there. The questions raised here are those which many teachers, parents and children often pose. A dialogic style has been chosen to make the book accessible and for easy understanding. Almost every page may stand by itself and when read in conjunction with its collateral section, may also be part of a larger argument. Since the text is divided into sections meant for different kinds of readers, a certain degree of repetition was unavoidable. But that should not trouble any but the most thorough of critics, since even when the same issue is being discussed for another kind of reader, distinctive facets have inevitably emerged.

agree?

Finally, there is a larger and bolder purpose behind the writing of this book. Too often, debates on education, textbooks and curricula have been limited to narrow circles of experts. These debates deserve to go much beyond such confines. As we argue elsewhere in this book, reposing too much faith in experts is dangerous. It is essential that teachers, parents and young people join the debate. These are not simple issues and we have tried to be true at least to the spirit of their complexity. The participation of those to whom education matters the most should not be through simplifications. We hope that this book will serve as an invitation to greater involvement with educational change and thence to social change in India.

ACKNOWLEDGEMENTS

Ashok R. Chandran of SAGE shaped this book in many ways. In a sense it had begun several years ago, while the authors were struggling with writing, translating and criticizing social science school textbooks, but Ashok yanked it to the forefront of our lives, pressing home to us the need for it. He sculpted it at every level, from insisting that we use a pleasant question and answer format to cutting out verbose pontifications to helping us visualize the typical reader. In the process, we gained a tremendous respect for Ashok's commitment and abilities. After he became preoccupied with his own research and creative writing, Rekha Natarajan took over, and despite her many other responsibilities, helped us cross the last hurdles and bridges. Her support and guidance were invaluable. We are grateful to the anonymous reviewer for detailed and useful comments, as well as Sushmita Banerjee who quickly piloted the final manuscript through production.

While writing this book it was driven home again and again to us that there is no such thing as authorship by individuals. What we have said comes from several sources, which themselves exist in deep overlapping layers. There were many 'elders' who gathered around Eklavya, Madhya Pradesh, and guided us on our way to learning about textbooks and the social sciences. Arvind Sardana, Rashmi Paliwal, C.N. Subramaniam, Kamal Mahendroo, Sushil Joshi and Anjali Noronha have engaged with school textbooks more than anyone else in the country. They taught us through their praxis. From our university days we have been listening to, reading and, most of all, observing the personal examples set by Avijit Pathak, Krishna Kumar and the late Sureshchandra Shukla. Sonam Wangchuk and Rebecca Norman at SECMOL, Ladakh, as well as K.J. Baby and Shirly Joseph at Kanavu, Kerala, provided us a diverse set of experiences. The distinct natures of these institutions and the lived experiences of these people helped us to understand many things. Yogendra Yadav and Sarada Balagopalan at the Centre for the Study of Developing Societies helped us to appreciate the new trends emerging at the NCERT.

We are grateful to the NCERT, SECMOL and Eklavya for granting us permission to include some of the pages of their textbooks. Alex would like to thank his family for allowing him to remain footloose. Amman is grateful to Kabir, Kalyani, Zubaidah and Kulwant Madan for keeping him tied down and focused.

The royalties from this book are pledged to Adharshila Learning Centre, an alternative place of learning at Sendhwa, Madhya Pradesh. Adharshila is asking difficult questions: What kind of education can build a just and humane society? Can schools build good human beings and not just submissive workers for a global economy? Are schools destined only to make people blind to the unfairness of their society? Adharshila helps keep alive our hope in education.

PARENTS

Examinations and Careers

1   **In India, the child participates in state-level and national-level exams for securing admission in good colleges or getting a job. How will these textbooks help my child? I am concerned.**

Many parents, educators and students are aware of the damage caused by the pressure of such competitive exams. The student, instead of enjoying what she learns, is forced to focus only on what the examination requires and how best to satisfy that. In standard 12, this mania centres round sciences and mathematics, because of the competitive 'entrance' exams for joining engineering and medical courses. Fortunately, social sciences at schools do not suffer from the same fate. Those who learn and teach social sciences can therefore focus on getting young people to understand life—its social dimensions and challenges.

2   **May be not in standard 12, but those who study social sciences too appear for competitive exams later in life. For science students too, there are competitive exams later with a social science component.**

Yes, like the civil services examination, or the entrance exams of some universities and for social work courses. But they usually call for special preparation at that age (around or after graduation) and do not rely directly on the school curriculum. Those who prepare for the civil services exam in India use school textbooks, but these books are only a part of the larger set of books they read.

The objective of a textbook is not to prepare students for a particular type of competitive exam, but to help students face challenges in their adult lives. This is not to say that the new textbooks will not help in competitive exams later in life. But three or five years after leaving school, students may not retain much of the factual details they read years ago. The new textbooks would have equipped them in terms of attitudes, and ways to analyse issues. The competitive exams too may change, in their type and pattern. The new textbooks popularize an approach that makes students skilled and flexible (see Extracts 1.1 and 1.2). The new textbooks will develop students' ability to put forward an argument, analyse a situation, or summarize and debate information given to them.

3 **How do the new textbooks help students face challenges in their adult lives?**

Students should begin to enjoy thinking and enquiring about the social sciences—that is the aim of the new textbooks. In this process, the students also internalize a repertoire of concepts and knowledges, which they can deploy in various situations in real life. In contrast, students who slog only to memorize facts will be at a loss when asked to apply in real life what they have learnt. Typically, the memorizers freeze when they face the same issue (whether in an examination hall or in the world outside) from a different angle, or in a different language.

Parents Helping Kids at Home

4 **I did not study social sciences after school and I barely remember what was there in the text-books. Will I be able to use the new textbooks while teaching my child?**

Yes, certainly. These textbooks discuss everyday social, political and economic scenes. Compared to the earlier textbooks, the new textbooks are much more inviting for parents who wish to be involved in their child's education. The new textbooks are readable and easy to understand, and a parent can actively participate in the child's learning.

Question 103

Extract 1.1
Learning to Think

You are an artisan standing on a tiny wooden platform held together by bamboo and rope fifty metres above the ground. You have to place an inscription under the first balcony of the Qutb Minar. How would you do this?

Source: NCERT history textbook, *Our Pasts II*, standard 7, p. 57.

Extract 1.2
Broadening their Vision

Imagine

Babur and Akbar were about your age when they became rulers. Imagine you have inherited a kingdom. How would you make your kingdom stable and prosperous?

Source: NCERT history textbook, *Our Pasts II*, standard 7, p. 73.

How can parents help? The new textbooks encourage students to explore the world outside and connect it with what is written in the chapters. In this, parents—especially educated parents—can help the child. Parents who are not highly educated can encourage the child by sharing their own views of events. If parents start enjoying the textbooks, that may help children look at their own textbooks and studies positively.

5   **If you have changed a lot of things, then it will be difficult for us parents, who are used to the older pattern, to adjust to the new books.**

Definitely not! On the contrary, you might start enjoying schooling! The new textbooks are written in a style that any child can understand. All you need to do is to spend time with the child, think about the concepts and encourage the child to think instead of learning by rote.

6   **Do you mean to say that a parent from any subject specialization can help the child use the new textbooks?**

Subject specialization helps. A parent who has studied economics will have an edge while helping the child learn economics. Similarly, if the parent is an agriculture officer, she can comfortably discuss the government's agricultural policies. Or if the parent is working in the mining industry, she can help with geography lessons. That is natural. But subject specialization is not essential. Every parent will find something or the other that he or she can add to the child's learning experience. As a parent who has lived longer than the child and seen more of the world, you might come up with more answers or a different answer. Do not dismiss what the child says, but make her aware of various other possibilities.

7   **Does helping my child also mean that I have to do his 'projects' for him? In my neighbourhood, one person sells the projects.**

'Projects' are assigned to the child because activities (not just passive reading) enable the child to learn things well. So, you should not do the activity all by yourself for your child, or purchase a ready/finished project from a shop. You

Box 1.1

Teaching through Activities

Teachers need to understand how to plan lessons so that children are challenged to think and to try out what they are learning, and not simply repeat what is told to them. A new problem is that in the name of 'activities' and 'play way' methods, a lot of learning is being diluted by giving children things to do that are far below their capability.

One concern is that, a focus on activities would become too time consuming, and make greater demands on teachers' time. Certainly, doing activities requires that time be spent in planning and preparing for activities. Initially, teachers need to make an effort to establish the classroom culture for activities and to establish the rules that will govern the space and use of materials.

Source: Excerpted from the National Curriculum Framework 2005.

should participate to help the child, but let him/her benefit from the activity.

In India, we have not fully explored this method of learning social sciences. Also, it might be easier to design meaningful activities in some subjects than in others (see Box 1.1). The new textbooks try to ensure that the activities are challenging but within the reach of the child.

8   What roles are parents expected to play?

The parent is to be a resource person, who has experienced, read and heard about the social, political and economic events happening around the child. The parent is expected to be an active discussant and participant in the learning of the child. Parents' sharing of experiences or awareness will help the child adapt to the needs of the textbook.

9   How do the 'projects' and 'activities' help the child?

Parents can contribute in such 'learning by playing'. Not all concepts in the social sciences can have such physical, manifest models, but discussions and examples can be used in many ways. Political science or economics textbooks ask students to collect information of events around them (see Extract 1.3). The history textbook asks children to imagine and write about events mentioned in the textbook. These help the child understand and evaluate events.

The National Politics of Textbooks

10   When a political party comes to power, it changes textbooks prepared under the previous regime. Politicians are ruining the future of children.

It is not fair (or correct) to view the new textbooks in that vein. Yes, the decision to produce new textbooks emerged out of the United Progressive Alliance (UPA) government's belief that the previous government (the National Democratic Alliance [NDA] government) had inserted its own ideologies into school textbooks. And yes, there was unprecedented political support given to taking a fresh look at school textbooks.

ACTIVITY 3

One way to find out if adults are undernourished is to calculate what nutrition scientists call Body Mass Index (BMI). This is easy to calculate. Take the weight of the person in kg. Then take the height in metres. Divide the weight by the square of the height. If this figure is less than 18.5 then the person would be considered undernourished. However, if this BMI is more than 25, then a person is overweight. *Do remember that this criterion is not applicable to growing children.*

Let each student in a class find out the weight and height of three adult persons of different economic backgrounds such as construction workers, domestic servants, office workers, business-persons etc. Collect the data from all the students and make a combined table. Calculate their BMI. Do you find any relationship between economic background of person and her/his nutritional status?

Source: NCERT, economics textbook, *Understanding Economic Development,* standard 10, p. 13.

The political decision was followed by several educational decisions. India's National Policy on Education provides for evaluating the National Curriculum Framework every five years. For a long time it had been acknowledged that there were problems in the content and methods of teaching children, including in the NCERT textbooks. But reforms were slow to happen. The call for a fresh look presented an opportunity for large-scale changes. The new textbooks

Question 40–53

should be seen as an attempt to address some of the issues in teaching children. Sensing the opportunity, many top-notch academics participated in the writing of textbooks.

| | Textbooks are changed every few years because of conflicts between political parties and their ideologies. Are the new textbooks any different?

The new textbooks are different in that they try to re-fashion the way teachers and students interact in the classroom. In the context you mention, the most debated is the history textbook; so, let us see how it has evolved.

All historians—whether nationalist, Marxist or Hindutva—have their own interpretations of historical events. Each group can find examples and information to re-create or re-interpret the subject in line with their respective ideology. In textbooks, each can list out the events that matter most in their own ideological framework and replace one set of national heroes with another.

There were debates on how many sentences in the history textbook should be on the Aryans, Ashoka, Alexander, Akbar or Aurangzeb. So, as governments changed (and textbooks changed), the number of sentences on historical events and characters changed. But all along, there was no change or debate on the role of textbooks, their place in the classroom or their impact on examinations. Children were supposed to just memorize the information given in the textbook and reproduce it in the examination.

The new textbooks have resulted from another question—how can textbooks reshape interaction between teachers and students in the classroom, so as to encourage students to think and weigh arguments (instead of only memorizing facts). So, while the earlier textbook writers debated whether to include particular bits of information ('Did the people of Rig Vedic society eat beef?'), and their decision was guided by ideological preferences, the writers of the new textbooks focused on the learning of history—what is history, how does one learn about the past, what are the complexities, how does a historian work amidst them, and so on. The writers of the new textbooks, as they wrote, repeatedly asked themselves, 'Is this relevant? Should the child learn this?' The objective was not to merely balance various political interests.

Box 1.2

In Kerala, Questions are in the New Style

An annual examination for class 7 had only nine questions—all 'activities'. See how the questions test the child's understanding, and not memory.

Activity 1

Endosulfan tragedy, scarcity of drinking water in Plachimada and Chikunguniya fever are three instances of social problems that emerged in our society due to the faulty development perspective. Make a table to show the ways in which soil, water and air are polluted in our surroundings.

Activity 2

The table below shows the budget of a country:

Sector	Budget allocation
Health	120 crore
Education	150 crore
Housing	100 crore
Defence	630 crore

(a) Do you consider this budget to be welfare-oriented for the people? Why?

(b) What could be the reasons for allocating more money towards defence?

(c) Re-allocate the budget to make it welfare-oriented for the people.

Activity 3

Here are some news headlines of recent events. Classify them into ruling systems.

- Army captures power.
- Government calls for a meeting with organizations on strike and demanding higher salary.
- King Gyanendra to quit. Power to the people.
- United Front gains power with two-thirds majority.
- Saudi King dies, son takes over.
- Military coup in Fiji.

Source: From the annual examination question paper of standard 7, social science, Kasargod, Kerala.

Different Boards and Compatibility between Them

12 In the Indian school system, there are different streams, that is, different regional and national education 'boards' to which schools are affiliated. What will happen if I move to a new state, and my child joins another stream in that state? Will there be problems because my child was using the new textbooks?

We advise you to select a school that emphasizes the child's active learning rather than rote learning.

When the child shifts from one school board to another, she will be forced to adjust to some new ways—rules, textbooks, language, and so on. If your child was using the new textbooks of the NCERT, she might face one problem. With the introduction of the new NCERT textbooks, the gap in quality between the NCERT books and those of some state boards has widened. Until those state boards catch up, your child will have to adjust to the old-style textbooks there. The good news is that some state boards are already using new-style textbooks and examinations (see Box 1.2) that emphasize skill-building over information-building. Sooner or later, all school boards will move towards better models of teaching children and new-style textbooks.

Another textbook problem that the child will face is one due to a move from the NCERT to a state board and which was prevalent even in the case of old textbooks. State boards usually emphasize local heroes in history textbooks; the NCERT textbooks are less state-centric. Tipu Sultan or Shivaji would be a 'benevolent ruler' in one state board's textbook, an 'invader' in another state board's textbook, but in the NCERT textbook, neither. The child might therefore take some time to adjust to the textbooks in the new environment. This problem is not because of the new NCERT textbooks, but due to differences in the textbooks prepared by various state boards. But this is a minor problem. There will be continuities and commonalities too across textbooks.

Box 1.3

Using Local Contexts in Schools

Let us briefly see what happened in Operation New Hope. It was primarily aimed at classes 1 to 5 in Ladakh.

In this region of Jammu and Kashmir, till the late 1990s, less than 10 per cent of the students passed the national board exams in class 10.

Why? Because education was in Urdu or English (languages unfamiliar to the children of Ladakh), and the national-level textbooks the students used did not relate to the children's social surroundings. These books described the ocean currents and monsoons, rainforests and mangroves; to children living in Ladakh—a cold desert created by a rain-shadow—these elements were alien.

The new learning materials developed under Operation New Hope for primary school replaced the counting of unfamiliar coconut trees, rabbits, peacocks and mangoes with what the children saw around them: yaks, apricots, black-necked cranes and cheese.

Their histories and close interactions with Lhasa or their being a part of the Silk Route had never been in national textbooks. The new books could incorporate such elements (See Extracts 1.5 and 1.6). The new books also described how the unique geographical features demanded special adjustments and influenced the way they built networks with the rest of the world, and how they evolved.

Please give the child time to adjust to the new environment and study material.

Textbook Reform All over the Country

13 **Have such textbooks been used elsewhere in the country?**

There have been many attempts to bring out improved, child-centred school textbooks in India. For instance, the last two decades have seen radical changes in the textbooks of Kerala. The old-style dull, incomprehensible books have also begun to gradually disappear in Chhattisgarh and Assam. There have been subject-specific initiatives in the sciences and social sciences by Eklavya in Madhya Pradesh (see Extract 1.4). Similar innovations can be seen in the Krishnamurthy Foundation's packages for various upper-primary classes and in Digantar's work in the primary schools of Rajasthan. Most Indian states have felt the pressure to improve school textbooks and have dabbled in various experiments (see Box 1.3). These programmes have included not only developing new materials for students, but also training, enabling and helping teachers to use the new materials in schools.

14 **Are the new NCERT textbooks different from these kinds of efforts?**

The new NCERT textbooks draw upon the experiences and learnings of all these books. Many people involved in the innovative efforts in various states participated in the NCERT's project and enriched the quality and depth of the new textbooks. Still, the new textbooks are different in two respects.

First, the new NCERT textbooks are aimed at being used all over India, not in any one state. In many states (Goa, Sikkim and Haryana, to name just three), there are no separate textbooks other than those published by the NCERT.

Second, while there were changes in the state-level textbooks of some states, they continued to largely follow the National Curriculum Framework of 1986 and the syllabus suggested under it. The new NCERT textbooks follow the National

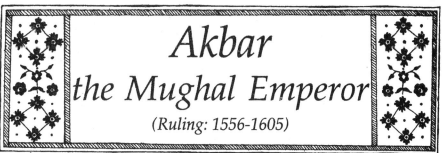

CHAPTER 1

Akbar
the Mughal Emperor
(Ruling: 1556-1605)

The Beginning of Mughal Rule in India

This picture shows a Mughal army ready for battle. The soldiers have several new kinds of weapons that are not seen in the pictures of earlier times. Can you identify them?

Such was the army of the Mughal emperor Babar (बाबर). Babar had been ruling in Afghanistan and he was trying to conquer more lands. At that time Delhi was being ruled by the Afghan king, Sultan Ibrahim Lodi. In 1526 the armies of Babar and Lodi had a battle at Panipat, north of Delhi. With the help of their cannons and guns, Babar's army dealt a crushing defeat to the Delhi Sultan.

After taking a lot of riches from the treasuries of the Indian kings, Babar's soldiers wanted to return to Afghanistan. But Babar wanted to stay on and

AKBAR 3

Source: Eklavya textbook, *Social Studies*, standard 8, part 1, p. 3.
Note: The exercise of examining this illustration made children more sensitive to historical changes in technology. Illustrations were not being used only to fill spaces and look pretty.

Extract 1.5
Local Contexts: Everyday Work in Kashmir

there. There are also many farmers in the region, but the valley is especially famous for its craftspeople. For centuries, people in Kashmir have been making fine handicrafts. They make shawls, felt, and carpets out of materials such as wool, pashmina, silk, and cotton. Some craftspeople weave beautiful baskets of thin pieces of willow. Some are very skilled at making tables and boxes of walnut wood. Beautiful containers and plates are made out of papier mâché. Metalworkers make elegant samovars out of brass.

Can you complete these statements?

Wool and cotton are used to make _____

Baskets are made of _____

Papier mâché is made of _____

Samovars are made of _____

Now let's read about some carpet weavers.

Ali and Abdullah are sitting in front of a loom. Wool strings are tied from top to bottom. The boys' hands move quickly along these strings. They hold a small, curved blade in one hand. There are many different coloured wool balls hanging above their heads.

A man is sitting to the side. This is Ustad. He reads out loud and the weavers recite with him. Can you guess what they are saying? Ustad has the design of the carpet drawn on a piece of graph paper. It tells what colour of wool should be used and where the knot should be made. Ali and Abdullah follow the instructions. They push some

Source: Jammu and Kashmir State Board of Education textbook, *Environmental Studies, Part I for Class IV: A Textbook of Science for Children of Ladakh*, pp. 75–76.

Curriculum Framework (NCF) of 2005 and its syllabus, which are very different from the earlier framework and syllabus.

15 What had been the impact of the earlier innovations in various states?

Overall, there was a better quality of learning. Students found the innovative books easier to read and understand. Teachers found the books to have more examples and simpler language, and hence easier to use in the classroom. Officials and

wool between the strings, pull it through and knot it. Then they cut it with their blade.

After the weaving is complete, they wash the carpet. This makes the colours bright. Then they cut the wool level with scissors and knot the strings at the end.

Making a carpet takes many days of hard work. A large carpet takes more than two months. A carpet can have a hundred or a thousand knots in one square inch, an area as big as this. The more knots, the higher the quality. Carpets with many knows last for many years.

Have you seen carpets at home? Are they woven in Kashmir? What other types of carpets are available in Ladakh?

What happens after the carpet is finished? The wool and the loom do not belong to Ustad or the weavers. They belong to a trader. The trader lets Ustad and the weavers use them. He pays them a daily wage. He tells them what design to make. When the carpet is finished, he sells it in big markets in India or other countries.

Kashmiris have been weaving carpets for five or six hundred years. It is said Sultan Zain ul Abidin brought carpet weavers from Persia to teach their craft to the Kashmiris.

Jammu region

The main city of Jammu region is Jammu. In the city, people have many different occupations, but in the villages, most people depend on farming. We will now read about some Jammu farmers.

Unlike Ladakh, villages in Jammu are close together. In villages the houses are close to each other. Most villages are also larger than

Source: Jammu and Kashmir State Board of Education textbook, *Environmental Studies, Part I for Class IV: A Textbook of Science for Children of Ladakh*, pp. 75–76.

non-governmental organizations visited the innovating states and tried out similar improvements in their own states. Almost everywhere the feeling was, 'This is the right direction to move.' The new books had more and better images, and sections that retained the child's attention in the classroom. Scholarly studies that evaluated the textbooks praised the efforts.

But these innovations were scattered and the question was 'if such textbooks are good, why does not the NCERT also follow the same approach?'

16 Well, now the NCERT has also moved in that direction.

Yes, the NCERT has a special status in India and is considered the highest authority on what should (or should not) be taught. We expect that the NCERT example will encourage all states to make even bigger and more wide-ranging changes in their own textbooks.

17 But were there problems in the states due to the innovative textbooks?

The biggest problem was that they were new. Teachers were used to the old approach and were comfortable with it. Initially, they were unsure of how to use the new textbooks. But some teacher-training sessions and introductions to the basic philosophy of the innovative textbooks helped. After initial hiccups, teachers began to report that the children enjoyed these textbooks much more and learnt better than before.

Many teachers felt that their own workload had increased. They agreed that the new ways of teaching would benefit the students, but were unhappy about the effort (they thought) they had to make in the classroom. They also feared that reviewing homework would be tougher in the new approach. This teacher-workload problem remains an issue, especially in schools that are understaffed and where teachers are over-worked or asked to do various non-teaching activities along with their routine work.

Question 94

Across states, the best resolution to this uneasiness came from the students themselves. When teachers saw the significant difference the textbooks had made in their students, they resisted less.

18 The textbooks will be used only in a few schools and not in all the schools of the country. Is it fair to 'try' the new books on one set of students, while other students (who will compete with them later in life) are not subjected to such 'experiments' or 'trials'? Will this affect their competitiveness?

Nowadays, most children attend coaching classes to prepare for competitive examinations. These classes drill the students in the pattern of questions expected in that particular exam. However, if the exam organizers change the pattern of questions, such children will find themselves lost.

In contrast, the new NCERT textbooks raise the basic quality of the child's learning. Children who have studied the new NCERT textbooks will bring to the examination hall a deeper understanding of things and a more active way of thinking. All else being equal, such students will have an edge over others in competitive examinations. They will also be better placed to face challenges in real life.

19 Do school teachers in India have the skills or the attitude to use the new textbooks?

The best institutions preparing professional teachers support the well-established skills and attitudes required for teaching the new NCERT textbooks. For instance, you will find this in the excellent Bachelor in Elementary Education (B.El.Ed.) programme run in several colleges in Delhi. Similar principles and practices are taught in the Bachelor of Education (B.Ed.) programme of the Central Institute of Education of the University of Delhi and several other places. In the earlier state- and local-level initiatives, teacher-training was a part of the textbook reform programme. Through training, teachers were re-oriented and familiarized with the new and innovative approach.

But teacher education in India, in general, is on a weak foot. Many B.Ed. centres and courses are ineffective in equipping teachers to be more child-centred, or to meaningfully engage with the children in a classroom. It is clear to all that we cannot stop with merely developing a better set of textbooks. Teacher education too needs to be revamped across the country.

Meanwhile, for the new textbooks, national-level teacher training has been visualized. Also, in most new textbooks, there are instructions to teachers on how to use the books in the classroom. The NCERT has brought out a sourcebook for teaching and learning in primary schools. It has also held video conferencing with the Regional Institutes of Education. Resource books for teachers in middle and high schools will probably be brought out.

20 What problems are teachers likely to face while teaching the new textbooks?

First, teachers will realize that their old way of teaching is insufficient. The objective of the earlier textbooks was to enable children to recall facts and figures. The emphasis of the new textbooks is on developing the child's thinking capabilities. So, it is not enough for the teacher to possess lots of information; she too must think actively such that her students develop their own thinking abilities.

Second, the teacher is likely to face difficulty due to the newness of the text. It will take time to get acquainted with the new materials, methods and examples in the textbooks. The teacher is expected to use a textbook to engage the students and stimulate their thoughts. The textbook is not merely a bundle of information to be read aloud and explained in an information-filling manner. So the teacher herself has to read the textbook, resolve her own problems with the text, and then use it with the students.

Third, the teacher is likely to face a workload problem. Checking identical answers can be done quickly and easily. In the new textbooks, there are many open-ended scenarios where various children are expected to write different answers (there is no 'single, correct' answer). Reading diverse answers and checking whether students have grasped the concepts takes more time and effort. In this situation, the teacher's task as an evaluator will not be as easy as it was in the past. On the other hand, teachers would now enjoy teaching more (see Extract 1.7).

See also the chapter on Teachers

Extract 1.7
E-mail from a Teacher

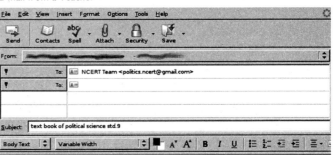

My name is A..., I am a social science teacher working in .... School, B.... I would like to congratulate you on the really thought provoking book you have brought out for std.9. I have been a social science teacher for about 16 years and it used to take all my creative abilities to make "civics" interesting!!! With your wonderful book the students actually wait for a poltical science class.
Your idea of beginning the lessons with examples, particularly the way you have dealt with Chapter One on Democracy in the Contemporary World - set the pace for my political science classes. Now it's more of a discussion than "I teach, you listen" kind of class. And for this I have the authors of this book to thank. One little grouse though, I can't finish my portions on time!!!
Keep up the good work! I am sure because of your efforts, our children will grow to be politically conscious and aware of their rights and duties as citizens of India.
With regarda,
A.

Source: The NCERT political science textbooks team.

21 Many school teachers may have educational qualifications but are not interested in teaching the subject in an exciting manner. They do not share the enthusiasm of the textbook writers. What can parents do in such situations?

Perhaps one must not blame the teachers too much for this situation. There are too many odds against which teachers struggle—tyrannical principals, low salaries, poor social recognition, continuously racing against time in the classroom, carrying work home, and so on. Parents should therefore compliment and complement the efforts of teachers.

Luckily, a parent can inspire the child, in many ways. And as a parent, you will find the new textbooks easier to read than the old textbooks. The new textbooks contain several examples from everyday life; they are not dense paragraphs of information that can be deciphered only with some theoretical understanding of the subject.

Please spend time with your child, and together, go through the textbooks. Discuss the examples. While your child does the activities asked in the textbooks, sit along with her. Reluctant teachers (the kind you are worried about) usually skip the activities or tackle them without seriousness. But it is through such activities and examples that the child develops her understanding (see Extract 1.8). Remember that participating in such learning processes is also a great way to spend evenings together; it is more fun than watching television programmes and advertisements with her.

22 Why do I need to study the social sciences? People grow up and find out these things by themselves, don't they?

Yes, people usually learn from their experiences in daily lives. Such learning can be profound but it can also be disjointed and incomplete. They may not find out some things at all. Take for example, the widespread sympathy for the idea of dictatorship. When frustrated, many feel that democracy is a noisy and dirty affair, and perhaps it would be better to live under a dictator. But have these people lived under a dictator? Wouldn't they like to have some control over the local politician?

In this case, it will help if we systematically study democracy's benefits and problems. That way we will prize more dearly what we have and work hard towards realizing

LET'S WORK THESE OUT

Discuss the following situations:

1. Look at the picture on the right. What should be the developmental goals for such an area?

2. Read this newspaper report and answer the questions that follow:

> A vessel dumped 500 tonnes of liquid toxic wastes into open-air dumps in a city and in the surrounding sea. This happened in a city called Abidjan in Ivory Coast, a country in Africa. The fumes from the highly toxic waste caused nausea, skin rashes, fainting, diarrhoea etc. After a month seven persons were dead, twenty in hospital and twenty six thousand treated for symptoms of poisoning.
>
> A multinational company dealing in petroleum and metals had contracted a local company of the Ivory Coast to dispose the toxic waste from its ship.

(i) Who are the people who benefited and who did not?

(ii) What should be the developmental goal for this country?

3. What can be some of the developmental goals for your village, town or locality?

Source: NCERT economics textbook, *Understanding Economic Development,* standard 10, p. 7.

Extract 1.9
Questions that Connect to Reality

I have heard a different version. Democracy is **off** the people, **far** (from) the people and (where they) **buy** the people. Why don't we accept that?

Source: NCERT political science textbook, *Democratic Politics,* standard 9, p. 24.

---

its potential. After all, a dictator rules as he wishes; it is only in a democracy that the rulers are forced to pay attention to people's wishes.

23 Are not these books a kind of government propaganda, trying to give a goody-goody picture of government and democracy?

The new textbooks are full of open-ended questions. Take for example the *Democratic Politics* textbook for standard 9. Here is a twist to Abraham Lincoln's famous definition of democracy (see Extract 1.9).

Is that a goody-goody picture?

24 Hmm...the cartoon on page 34 of that textbook is very sad and cynical. It shows a Canadian saying, 'We voters are angry and we're not going to take anymore. The Liberals have been arrogant. They've broken our trust in government. They stole our money. So, on June 28, we're going to do what Canadians do best. We're going to vote them back in.'

Yes. That cartoon was published in Canada just before the 2005 parliamentary elections, when everyone including the cartoonist, expected the Liberal Party to win again. But the Liberals lost that election. The textbook poses the question, 'Is this cartoon an argument against democracy or for democracy?' Yes, the cartoon is sad and cynical, but that is how many people feel when they look at the kind of democracy and political system they have, isn't it? The textbook tries to say that we cannot stop there. We have the choice and the chance to understand, and to improve matters.

25 Do we have to say such things to children?

The readers of the standard 9 book are in their teens. They know what is going on around them. Ask them about corruption in their town or village, and some might even tell you how much a local *neta* or official takes for getting some work done. Not to acknowledge things like corruption will make the children even more cynical. It is better to accept our reality and then search for the pathways of hope.

26 Where is the basis of hope? Our democracy seems mired in petty politics and corruption. No one seems to get justice and only the rich and the powerful flourish.

Yes, there is great injustice in our country—injustice in too many ways to count—in wealth, in gender, in community, in caste, and so on. And yes, when we look around, it seems difficult to sustain a sense of hope. When gutters are choked, politicians promise to clean them, but disappear only to make the same promise five years later. Our *babus* are corrupt and keep finding new ways to seek bribes. We ourselves sometimes discriminate against certain groups of people. We marginalize communities and push them into ghettoes, by our suspicion and our jibes.

Yet, the impression that things are static is false. Things are changing, slowly but surely. And one of the most important processes driving that change is democracy.

27 **Do you think we have really improved since India won her freedom?**

Yes, we have improved a lot since 1947. But our freedom is incomplete. Mahatma Gandhi pointed out that merely pushing out the British would not mean *swaraj*. *Swaraj* would come only when we learnt to rule ourselves. By winning freedom we commonly refer to freedom from the British. But actually our people continue to be largely unfree.

28 **What is freedom?**

That is a big question. Freedom is about being able to realize all your potential. It means being able to discover your talents and then being able to develop them fully. Its absence is easier to recognize. If a writer wishes to write in a certain way, but is told not to, we can see that her freedom is being curtailed. To a girl who is good in science, but goes to a badly equipped village school with ill-trained teachers, freedom is being denied. In an educated youth who is searching for but unable to get a job, we can see that freedom is missing. After all, we wanted freedom from the British because they were curtailing our growth.

29 **But textbooks cannot create freedom. You need political struggles, you need people to go out and get into face-offs with oppressors, you need big economic changes...**

Yes, you need all that. But without people who understand reality, where are you? Without people who speak up, face adversity with courage and penetrate lies, how can anything change? We need decency, honesty and courage. And those are the qualities that good school education encourages.

30 **You mean social science textbooks will do all this?**

Textbooks, especially the new ones, try to do this. Some parts work, some do not. The new textbooks encourage children to keep their minds open, learn to think freely and critically, and be constructive. The new textbooks prompt children to examine any question from as many angles as they can, and ask 'who benefits from a practice' (like one-person, one-vote) and 'who loses from it' (see Extract 1.10).

Equal right to vote

The story above begins with Kanta standing in line to cast her vote. Look again at the various people who are standing in line with her. Kanta recognises her employer, Ashok Jain and Chotte Lal, her neighbour. In a democratic country, like India, all adults irrespective of what religion they belong to, how much education they have had, what caste they are, or whether they are rich or poor are allowed to vote. This, as you have already read in the Class VI book, is called **universal adult franchise** and is an essential aspect of all democracies. The idea of universal adult franchise is based on the idea of equality because it states that every adult in a country, irrespective of their wealth and the communities she/he belongs to, has one vote. Kanta is excited to vote and happy that she is equal to all of the others because each of them has one vote.

But as her day goes on, Kanta becomes less certain about what this equality really means.

What is it that makes Kanta unsure? Let's take a look at a day in her life. She lives in a slum and has a drain behind her house. Her daughter is sick but she cannot take the day off from work because she needs to borrow money from her employers to take her child to the doctor. Her job as a domestic help tires her out, and finally she ends her day by again standing in a long line. This line, in front of the government hospital, is unlike the one in the morning because most of the people standing in it are poor.

Do you think Kanta has enough reason to doubt whether she really is equal? List three reasons from the story above that might make her feel like this.

Source: NCERT social science textbook, *Social and Political Life-II*, standard 7, p. 6.

A Constructive Approach

31 Talking about freedom without talking about duties makes me nervous.

Yes, it is futile to talk of freedom without duties. All of us should restrain ourselves in certain ways for freedom to exist. For freedom of speech, I should learn to speak, but also learn to keep quiet (while others are speaking). What is important is to learn why a duty is important. Merely following a duty because one is told to follow it will soon lead to enslavement. We should not encourage passivity or submissiveness. What we seek is a society where rules and regulations are carefully planned for the convenience and benefit of all. We seek a society where people are willing to re-examine whether the rules meet their purpose.

32 How can a teenager make out which duties are constructive and which are meant to control or manipulate?

Since there is no list of 'good' or 'bad' duties and rules, a good way is to keep your mind open, and learn to think freely and critically. Learn to examine any question from as many angles as you can, and ask who benefits from a practice (like 'one-person, one-vote') and who loses from it.

33 Why do we need open and critical thinking for being constructive?

We need to try out new ways of doing things that may give greater justice and freedom to our people. By emphasizing openness and critical thinking, we are more likely to become innovative and positive-thinking people. If people follow orders without understanding why the orders must be followed, or when people blindly imitate tradition, who will explore and experiment?

34 How can open thinking be taught?

One way to close people's minds is to have very few questions. Another way is to tell the student reader, 'Just learn the single, correct answer and repeat that answer in the examination. Don't think of anything else. Focus on the official answers.'

Instead, the new textbooks adopt an open approach (see Box 1.4). Look at the *Democratic Politics* textbook for standard 9. It has an unusually large number of questions at the end of

Box 1.4————————————

Questions to Encourage Thinking

The question 'What is democracy?' appears open-ended. But it is really not so because the textbook has given a definition ('democracy is a system of government in which...'), has explained it in one paragraph, and we have asked the student to write the 'official answer'. We are not encouraging her to think.

Instead, the new textbook adopts an open approach. It asks the student 'Consider the following facts about a country and decide if you would call it a democracy. Give reasons to support your decision.'

Such questions have no 'official answers' that the student can 'mug up'. Various students may give different answers. The question forces each student to weigh the facts, apply his understanding of 'what is democracy?', and arrive at a conclusion. In this way, the new textbook encourages open and critical thinking.

each chapter. In this textbook, there is often no single, correct answer to the questions in the chapters. What is important is for the student to understand what the ideas or concepts mean. She can then learn to apply that understanding and look at situations from various angles. The large number of questions gives students practice in thinking for themselves. The textbook avoids defining 'official questions' or offering 'official answers' for rote learning.

35 **Why should people learn to be critical? Isn't that a negative attitude?**

To be critical does not mean merely to point out flaws or to be cynical about everything. It has a deeper meaning, coming from the dialogues of Socrates, from the questioning of Prajapati by Indra in the *Aittriya Upanishad* and from the modern approach of trying to improve upon everything. It means asking questions to gain a deeper and higher understanding. Further, it means using that deeper understanding to ask how a better state of affairs can be created. For example, it means to ask why the panchayat should function through a committee, and why full powers should not be given only to the *sarpanch*. It means thinking through the dangers and the benefits. To be critical, in this sense, means to ask whether rules and procedures are doing their job and how we can improve upon them. It implies the comparing of alternative forms and a continuous search for a better state of affairs. This kind of critical approach is not cynically negative, but a necessary condition for being positive and constructive.

Just the Textbook Alone?

36 **Are you not expecting too much out of what are, after all, just textbooks?**

Yes, just reading a school textbook will not lead to all these changes (see Extract 1.11). Just reading about democracy is hardly enough to ensure that I will begin to practise it in my own life. If that had been true, then we should have been turning out ideal citizens in millions, from our schools. Often, our schools end up teaching bad civic attitudes—bow down before people in power, learn to live with irrational rules, be self-centred, do not care about what is happening around you, and so on.

Right against Exploitation

Once the right to liberty and equality is granted, it follows that every citizen has a right not to be exploited. Yet the Constitution makers thought is was necessary to write down certain clear provisions to prevent exploitation of the weaker sections of the society.

The Constitution mentions three specific evils and declares these illegal. First, the Constitution prohibits 'traffic in human beings'. Traffic here means selling and buying of human beings, usually women, for immoral purposes. Second, our Constitution also prohibits forced labour or begar in any form. 'Begar' is a practice where the worker is forced to render service to the 'master' free of charge or at a nominal remuneration. When this practice takes place on a life-long basis, it is called the practice of bonded labour.

Finally, the Constitution also prohibits child labour. No one can employ a child below the age of fourteen to work in any factory or mine or in any other hazardous work, such as railways and ports. Using this as a basis many laws have been made to prohibit children from working in industries such as beedi making, firecrackers and matches, printing and dyeing.

CHECK YOUR PROGRESS

On the basis of these news reports write a letter to the editor or a petition to a court highlighting the violation of right against exploitation:

A petition was filed in the Madras High Court. The petitioner said a large number of children aged between seven and 12 were taken from villages in Salem district and sold at auctions at Olur Nagar in Kerala's Thrissur district. The petitioner requested the courts to order the government to check these facts. **(March 2005)**

Children, from the age of five, were employed in the iron ore mines in the Hospet, Sandur and the Ikal areas in Karnataka. Children were forced to carry out digging, breaking stones, loading, dumping, transporting and processing of iron ore with no safety equipment, fixed wages and working hours. They handled a high-level of toxic wastes and were exposed to mine dust, which was above the permissible level. The school dropout rate in the region was very high. **(May 2005)**

The latest annual survey conducted by the National Sample Survey Organisation found that the number of female child labourers was growing both in rural and urban areas. The survey revealed there were 41 female child labourers per thousand worker population in rural areas as against the previous figure of 34 per thousand. The figure for male child had remained at 31. **(April 2005)**

DEMOCRATIC RIGHTS

105

Source: From NCERT political science textbook, *Democratic Politics*, standard 9, p. 105.

37 **What must accompany such textbooks if democracy is really to be encouraged?**

There must be workshops which sensitize teachers to the textbooks' key issues like freedom, equality and democracy. Teachers should read about issues, and meet each other to discuss and work out their own understandings. Alongside, there should take place a rethinking of the culture of the school so that it too teaches democratic values. That is why so many questions in the book are designed to lead toward reflecting upon the conditions that exist in the children's own schools. Teachers who themselves live in a very undemocratic environment can hardly be expected to exemplify healthy behaviour. We have schools that treat teachers like machines. Then why should we be surprised if students become regimented and cynical? Such a culture is the enemy of democracy. For a strong and healthy democracy, we need not just good textbooks, but also democratic schools.

38 **Is it not too much to expect that? I mean, it is difficult to run a school, and now, you are arguing for democracy in schools!**

Many people are moving in the direction of democratic education. People in government bodies like the NCERT keep asserting in their documents that good education is democratic education. People in non-governmental organizations like Eklavya, Digantar and Kerala Sastra Sahitya Parishad; in trusts like the ICICI Social Initiatives Group and Sir Ratan Tata Trust; in research organizations like the Home Bhabha Centre for Science Education and the Centre for Environment Education; and in many others—are trying to contribute to these changes in a variety of ways.

39 **Several of the new textbooks do not always give a rosy picture of India. In fact, they discuss social ills, political corruption and poverty. The old textbooks did not highlight such 'bad' things. Why is there a change now?**

School textbooks are written in a governmental-bureaucratic environment. People involved—bureaucrats, teachers and textbook writers—wish to avoid controversy. They fear that a government textbook which admits to corruption in India would be raised as an issue in Parliament. So, all play safe by talking about the rules of the present system, glossing over its weaknesses and discouraging any talk of alternative systems of governance.

Another reason is that textbook writers are sometimes ignorant of new and key debates in their subject. So they stick to traditional ideas and skip new topics and concerns. Sadly, in India, many leading experts have the attitude that writing textbooks is a cheap activity that reduces their prestige. But this time, the NCERT succeeded (to an extent) in roping in a much larger circle of experts, who boldly wrote about their subjects from a fresh perspective. By not talking about the problems of India, we actually weaken our children's education. Only when we are aware of our problems can we gird ourselves up to find their solutions.

Conflicts and Controversies Over Textbooks

40 **Whenever a new government is formed, the Opposition always complains that the ruling party's ideology is being put into the textbooks.**

Nowadays political parties show interest in school textbooks, much more than in the past. Their interest is usually in how the textbooks agree or differ with their own political ideology. Are their political heroes mentioned in the textbooks and what is said about them? Has anything unsavoury been said in the textbooks about certain communities? How have the textbooks presented the history and origins of India, and her various communities? These are what they ask. Typically, they raise questions of national or regional identity. Rarely do issues of education get addressed.

It is not only the political parties that ignite controversies. By filing public interest litigation, people drag the judiciary too into textbook controversies.

41 **Why cannot the experts just sit together and write whatever is true? These debates on what should or should not be taught in school are confusing.**

There is no agreement on what is 'true'. Education is all about cultural issues on which even serious thinkers have different points of view. For instance, should we teach children that consumerism is good for us, or should we teach that it is bad? It is consumerism that is creating so many new jobs. At the same time, it may be making us more prone to greed, jealousy and superficiality. So what should we teach about it? How do we want to portray modern industry and the economy?

42 **Are these questions so difficult to resolve? Have not experts already resolved them?**

In the first place, we do not have many 'experts' on these matters. We have a society where there is an increasing emphasis on technology and finance. In such a society, little

encouragement is given to developing a serious understanding and study of moral or social issues. Second, on
such issues, even the best scholars are not confident that
they are right.

43 **Why should the best scholars feel uncertain? They,
at least, should know what they are talking about.**

Knowledge is closely tied to our social life and the context in
which that knowledge is to be used. Let us consider, say, the
teaching of obedience to elders. This may make a lot of sense
in a society where little change is taking place and where
the elders always know considerably more than the young.
But in a society where change is taking place rapidly, the elders
may not know best. It is quite possible that the young may
pick up more useful ideas from elsewhere. In this situation
there may still be a person who insists that the knowledge
of the elders is right. It is possible that at an unconscious
level he may be wanting to uphold the authority of the older
generation.

The relation between a society's structure and knowledge
is especially tricky because it often operates below our
consciousness. Scholars studying culture and power have
explored this problem in detail. We usually realize only dimly
how much our social context affects our understanding.
The better scholars know this danger and are cautious of
sweeping judgements. It is quite difficult to be sure that
my stand is because I am right, and not because my social
experiences are making me see everything through tinted
lenses.

44 **Do you mean that each group, each class and each
caste sees things differently?**

No, they do not have a completely different view of the world
from each other. Many, if not most, understandings overlap
each other. The community I am part of, however, leaves a
deep impact on how I can see or understand various issues.
Consider if, for instance, my group's sense of identity rests
upon a hero who lived in the past. Suppose I discover some
evidence that he was also a human being, with the ordinary
weaknesses and failings of all human beings. My tendency
would be to find ways to ignore that evidence and to feel
uncomfortable about it. I would tend to continue to believe
what I held earlier. If somebody insisted on talking about
the failings of my hero, I would slip into a suspicion of the

motives behind the criticism. Perhaps they are intended to slight me, or my community...

45 **That may be possible when one is talking about history. But how can there be different group views on the government and current affairs?**

There is greater diversity of views on current affairs than on what happened in history. Suppose a piece of land is to be taken over by the government for building a dam or a factory. There can be several points of view. If I identify with those who are building the factory, then I may believe that it is good for the country and that it will lead to wealth and development, and so on. If I identify with those who are being evicted from their lands, I may believe that this is injustice, it is leading to the downfall of the country, it will lead to greater crime and unhappiness, and so on. The class or group I am part of will have some effect on what I believe. Of course, I can rise above all this and try to apply deeper and higher principles. But for that, I need to have internalized the idea of truth and the ways to move closer to it.

When one looks at current affairs, it is clear that there are different points of view. It is difficult to decide which one of them to support or which one to teach children.

46 **If there is such a difference of opinion among various groups, should not it be the duty of the government to decide what is right and teach only that?**

A government does not stand independent of or aloof from society. It is made up of people like you and me, who are more sympathetic to the interests of one group or the other. There is hardly any guarantee that the government will always only do what is right.

In the case of acquiring land for building a factory, for instance, the government may be closer to big industrialists than to small farmers. It would then tend to lean in one direction on grounds other than justice or fairness or development. However, a democratic government, which works in democratic ways by consulting various points of view, is less likely to display such behaviour. By the way, that is another big reason to support democracies—it is easier for them to avoid speaking only in the voice of one class or one community.

47 **Isn't there something called 'reality'? If we were to believe you, there would be no certainty left in the world.**

We do not mean to suggest that the world is a mirage swimming before our eyes. There is a reality behind all this. The tricky part, though, is finding out what exactly it is (see Extracts 1.12 and 1.13).

Extract 1.12
The World Upside Down?

Map 1
A section of the world map drawn by the geographer al-Idrisi in the twelfth century showing the Indian subcontinent.

Extract 1.13
Or, Is this the World Upside Down?

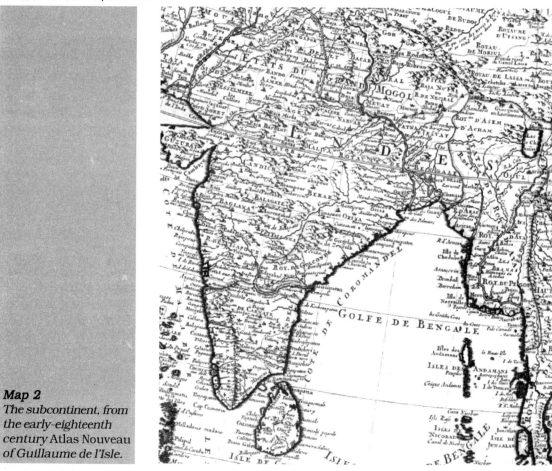

Map 2
The subcontinent, from the early-eighteenth century Atlas Nouveau of Guillaume de l'Isle.

Source: NCERT history textbook, *Our Pasts-II*, standard 7, p. 2.

There are many ways to discover reality. Science seems to lead them in reliability, but there is some merit in the other ways too. We cannot claim that science or any other way has reached the final truth. For that matter, this is one of the special characteristics of science—it accepts that it must always be incomplete. One seeks only a better approximation of the truth.

48 **Are you trying to say that all kinds of knowledge are equally true?**

Not at all. Not equally. Science-based knowledges are more trustworthy. They go through a process of extensive testing and must survive a process of being banged around by very critical reviewers. But we cannot argue that only the sciences have something worthwhile to say, or that only one method of science is suitable for all situations, or that there is nothing worth learning from other kinds of knowledge.

49 Humility and tentativeness may all be fine in the case of scholars, but no government can rule without an iron fist. Should not the government take a stand and enforce it?

On many matters, the government takes positions, makes laws and enforces rules. When the government is in a situation where the slightest delay can cause a disaster, it should indeed act immediately and without any half-heartedness. But should the government act like that all the time? One of the reasons why a democracy can provide a better government is that it calls upon the latter to consult widely and to reflect before it acts. On subjects like knowledge and scholarship, the government should not take a stand on every issue or bring about a law. Why should an iron fist imprison the human mind or advancement of knowledge?

Do we have 'reality' in science? How do we define a planet? Can the number of planets go up or down?

50 People cannot act wisely on their own. Don't governments have to act firmly?

To become people who act wisely, we should encourage a culture of reason and of dialogue. Most people talk about the importance of education for careers and for equality. Education is important for creating a better culture too. Through the social sciences, we can move towards a culture that uses reason, evidence and dialogue to decide matters.

51 Do you mean to say that I need to decide things on my own and not rely on experts?

We need people who have specialized knowledge. But we should also be able to understand what those experts say. Only then can we choose between competing advice from two experts, for instance. We need not yield control of our lives to others, however 'expert' they may be.

52 Is it inevitable that there will be politics and controversy over school textbooks?

Tugs of war are inevitable over what should or should not be said. Note that there are many issues here—between the interests of classes, on prioritizing the cultures of certain castes over others, on whether to treat the town superior to the village, on the portrayal of men and women, and so on.

When people talk about politics in the textbook, they forget all these and refer only to politicians who focus on a narrow range of issues (portrayal of government or ideologies). They hardly ever talk about other layers of politics in the school textbook—for example, whether to promote democracy or bury it under the dull teaching of rules and regulations.

53 **So, must one live with the idea of teaching only one partisan point of view?**

Not at all. One should strive to teach the truth to children. But that striving should reflect the nature of truth itself. It must embody tolerance of other points of view, as well as a primary focus on evidence and reason. It must encourage processes of dialogue and debate.

TEACHERS

Textbooks and Teacher Autonomy

54 Over the years, I have seen changes in the way I am expected to teach. What is expected of me by the new textbooks?

Yes, the way in which social science is taught has changed over the decades (see Box 2.1).

There can be two situations. Situation 1 is where textbooks are not used. Here, to gain information, the child is almost wholly dependent on the teacher's knowledge. Situation 2 is where there is too much emphasis on textbooks and the questions in them; the teacher loses all freedom and education becomes over-guided by examinations; and uniformity in evaluation. Even the child who gets good marks does not really learn.

Much is lost in these situations. In Situation 1, the teacher is able to provide examples or information relevant to the child, but we cannot be sure of the quality of what transpires in the classroom. In Situation 2, a rigid system of uniformity prevents the teacher from meaningfully interacting with the child in her social and environmental context. The new textbooks try to bridge the two problems—the textbooks ensure a certain quality but give space to the teacher.

55 There seems to be no teacher autonomy even in the new method to teach social science.

Like any textbook anywhere, the new textbooks too control the interaction between a teacher and a student. The textbook and the examination limit the ways a teacher transacts business in the classroom.

The ideal of teacher autonomy—a teacher determining the content and methods of teaching—remains a distant one. It calls for many interventions, not just designing better text-books. What is the reality?

1. In India, it is very difficult to get supporting materials that are child-friendly. Hence, a teacher in even a big city, leave alone other places, cannot equip herself with good materials for the class.

2. In India, teachers are expected to be proficient in teaching all social science subjects (school-level), irrespective of their subject specializations during graduation or higher studies. It is difficult for a teacher to identify and use relevant materials in each class or standard.

3. In India, teacher training or college education do not sufficiently equip students (that is, teachers of the future) to assess children's needs or imagine how a curriculum should be designed.

We believe that the new textbooks give space and freedom to a teacher to be creative and enterprising. At the same time, we are aware of external limits on the teacher's creativity.

56 **Why is it that the teacher has very little space for creativity in our schools today?**

Historically, schooling systems emerged in different ways in various countries. In many countries of Europe, schooling was not centralized till the nineteenth century. Children went to a teacher and learnt what the teacher thought was useful. Then as the state became powerful, it decided to regulate the education system through examinations. This made it necessary to have a certain uniformity across regions. That probably led to the current system of syllabi and textbooks. But in many of these countries, teachers continue to prepare the students in their own ways for the examinations. In India, examinations became the predominant driving force; a narrow focus on textbooks was seen as the only way in which examinations could be handled.

57 **So you agree that you cannot blame just the teachers for all this! After all, it is the examination that determines how we teach the children.**

Ha! Ha! Agreed. Before we discuss examinations, can we consider another aspect of your first question? How can the new textbooks be taught best? To understand how to teach, we must recognize what has changed. These are new types of social science books with very different content.

How to Teach

Changes in Content

58 **How has the content of the history textbook changed?**

History textbooks were largely chronological narratives. One would find the changing boundaries of empires and the successive dynasties of kings and queens. Their social, economic and religious policies and war strategies would be given, along with the dates and places sprinkled here and there. These details largely formed the content of the history textbooks. There was an underlying theme—critical treatment of colonial masters, but celebration of the freedom struggle and its heroes.

The new textbooks focus on basic processes of history:

1. Instead of kings and queens, the textbooks narrate the growth of agriculture and industry and how they changed people's lives. To understand processes, a few representative situations are examined and children are not burdened with exhaustive details of everything that happened everywhere. The belief is that children must understand the basic processes and not get lost in the details of who, when or where.

2. There is a sharper awareness of the lives of ordinary people, something which only rarely appeared in the old textbooks. What did people wear, what did they play, how did they live?

3. The underlying theme is the self-consciousness of the craft of a historian. The conventional way of teaching history was to present it as finished and final facts. Children never got a feel of how history was actually discovered and interpreted. The new textbooks focus on how history is written by historians. Children are introduced to how evidence is collected and examined, including how different evidences are weighed when they appear contradictory.

59 **What has happened to civics? Where did it go?**

Civics has been done away with and replaced by a *Social and Political Life* textbook (for the middle school) and *Political Science* and *Economics* textbooks (for the high school).

Box 2.2

Criticisms of the Old Civics

An enlightened mind accepts a principle only after examining it from several perspectives. This is the basis of science. It is also necessary that people examine their beliefs against the touchstone of reality. Compact and dense textbooks do not seem to be encouraging this. There is much scope for improvement in this regard. Critical engagement with ideas needs to be increased.

Source: 'The image of the citizen in NCERT's Civics textbooks', Amman Madan, *Shaikshanik Sandarbh*, May–June 1995, pp. 88–94.

One could add 'economic life' to the title of the middle-school book. In all of these, there is a shift in the way civics is taught.

Earlier, civics was largely a description of political institutions, with social and economic institutions mentioned here and there. Studying political institutions meant memorizing a long list of rules and regulations which formed the basis of these institutions (for example, powers and functions of the executive, qualifications of legislators). There was also an attempt to inform the child of all the good things that the government did to tackle various problems in society since independence. Yet, despite trying to inform the child in such painful detail, little got translated into daily life. The child found it difficult to identify with the processes talked about because little of that information matched the politics she observed around herself. Students and teachers complained that the civics textbook was the most 'textbookish'—distant and formal (see Box 2.2).

In the new textbooks, there is a shift of focus from rules towards basic principles. The assumption is that if children can understand the basic principles—like equality, diversity, and democracy—which underlie India's Constitution and should guide public life, then children will be better placed to understand the rules of the Parliament and the government. Details of rules and regulations have been reduced; instead, chapters focus on developing an understanding of the basic issues. Examples have been chosen from across the world to give children a wider and better perspective. Also, there are new chapters on dimensions of public life which are central to our daily existence, like the nature of economic life and the role played by the market. Children are taught to be conscious of the effects of the media and how the media affect the way we look at ourselves and the world.

60 Why were not the older textbooks as lively as the new ones?

Two reasons come to mind immediately:

1. The new textbooks are colourful and have lots of images, which have been used purposefully. In the past, resources to design textbooks were scarce. Today, it is easier to get visuals quickly. Similarly, printing books in colour but ensuring a reasonable price is possible now, unlike in the past

2. The new textbooks have benefited from many recent, smaller initiatives to design textbooks. So today, there are more specialists and more expertise in the designing of children's textbooks.

61 Geography looks much the same, though.

Yes, the geography textbooks of the NCERT have not changed as much as the others have. Compared to the new textbooks of the NCERT, the middle school textbooks designed by Lok Jumbish in Rajasthan and Eklavya in Madhya Pradesh have rethought more on how geography should be taught. The content, choice of images and the narrative style of NCERT's middle and high school textbooks are of the old pattern.

Question 113

Changing the Teaching Style

62 You have broadly described how the content of the textbooks has changed. How should teaching itself be changed?

So far, you have been teaching a subject in the following ways:

1. Lecturing—where, you speak and the children listen.

2. Reading out—where, you or a child reads the text aloud in the classroom.

3. Paraphrasing—where, in your own words, you paraphrase those textbook sentences which you consider important.

4. Underlining or bracketing—where, you ask the children to mark the important sentences in the textbook.

5. Dictating—where, you read aloud your own notes (typically, the answers to questions in the textbook) and ask the children to jot them down in their notebooks.

6. Reviewing—where, you ask the children to recall the answers or notes dictated by you.

These methods involve no real student-teacher interaction. They are teacher-led methods of learning. The only sound in the classroom is the teacher's, or a child nervously trying to answer questions asked by the teacher.

The new textbooks aim at active child participation in learning, by increasing student–teacher interaction. They promote student-to-student learning as well. The teacher is therefore expected to manoeuvre her classroom—its resources, its environment—and encourage children to think and learn, rather than accept whatever the teacher says. The children's sounds will fill the air as much as the teacher's.

63 Why is this important? Will this lead to better learning?

It is well established by scholars that a child learns best when she herself interacts with study materials, ideas or examples and tries to figure out what they mean to her. Learning improves when the child's active participation increases. When the child feels around an object or probes a concept, she develops a deeper and longer-lasting impression of it. Better learning also happens through listening to the narration of a historic event or of something which happened in another country.

Asking a provocative question, telling the child a stimulating joke—the possibilities are endless, and most good teachers already practise this. A student learns when she is treated like a friend (not a child) and feels respected.

Question 120

64 Yes, I too know this. The problem is that it takes a lot of time. What will happen to the course then? I have to cover the syllabus.

That dilemma has been around for years. We had textbooks with long and dense chapters, and the race was to finish teaching all that was in the textbook. At the same time, we know that children understand best when they (*a*) learn at their own pace and their interest is retained and (*b*) interact with, experience and explore what they learn.

How do we strike a balance between creating space for active participation and at the same time covering the entire textbook? Till now, to ensure a child's good performance in the examination, the balance was tilted towards completing the textbook. But now the textbooks and examinations have changed. The textbooks themselves are trying to give more space for interaction and dialogue. It is official now!

Box 2.3

Three Ways to Use 'In-between' Questions

1. Ask a child to respond to a question.

2. Form small groups, each of 5–7 children, who then work collectively and write answers. Ask them to create a poster or a chart of the answers.

3. Organize a group-wise presentation, develop team spirit. Ask the groups formed to express their views. If you notice differences in arguments, highlight them and encourage the groups to debate.

65   But this would mean chaos in the classroom.

No. If all that happens in the classroom is a lot of playing around by the children, then little learning will take place. What we now need to aim at is a new balance—through less lecturing and more dialogue with children.

66   How do these textbooks help in increasing the child's interaction with ideas?

Several elements of the new textbook have been introduced specifically to promote interaction. The new textbooks equip the teacher with many tricks and the teacher should use them to discourage passive listening and encourage active learning.

67   Tricks like what?

For instance, the new textbooks have various types of questions. One type is the 'in-between' question—questions placed between paragraphs of the main text itself. They are usually placed in such a way as to mark the end of a topic or a sub-section, within the main topic of discussion in a chapter. These questions provide the teacher with an opportunity to review the ideas discussed in that section (see Box 2.3). Teachers are expected to discuss all these questions to ensure that the children have understood the concept(s) discussed in that section.

The in-between questions themselves are of different types:

1. Some to stimulate a discussion which will take the students' attention to things that may not be fully explored in the text.

2. Some to introduce a new idea or link the current section with the next.

3. Some which review and summarize the concepts discussed in the section.

4. Some that compare what was discussed in the previous section with things happening around them.

68   The photographs and pictures too can be used for student participation in the classroom.

Exactly. That is why the images are there. The visuals in the new textbooks are not fillers—they are not a pretty way to occupy empty space, but are central to what is taught. The visuals explain concepts, pose critical comments, summarize ideas, provide evidences, evoke wonder, and so on (see Extract 2.1).

As you have been 'reading' the text and interpreting its words, you should 'read' the images as well. Do not pass them over; give time to the children to enjoy them. Let these images evoke greater curiosity and attention (see Extract 2.2). This will not only keep the child attentive, but will also deepen her understanding and learning. The class may suddenly sound very quiet, but that is because the children are

Extract 2.1
Pictures to Ponder About

IMPACT OF GLOBALISATION IN INDIA

In the last fifteen years, globalisation of the Indian economy has come a long way. What has been its effect on the lives of people? We look at some of the evidence.

Globalisation and greater competition among producers - both local and foreign producers - has been of advantage to consumers, particularly the well-off sections in the urban areas. There is greater choice before these consumers who now enjoy improved quality and lower prices for several products. As a result, these people today, enjoy much higher standards of living than was possible earlier.

Among producers and workers, the impact of globalisation has not been uniform.

Firstly, **MNCs** have increased their investments in India over the past 15 years, which means investing in India has been beneficial for them. MNCs have been interested in industries such as cell phones, automobiles, electronics, soft drinks, fast food or services such as banking in urban areas. These products have a large number of well-off buyers. In these industries and services, new jobs have been created. Also, local companies supplying raw materials, etc. to these industries have prospered.

Source: NCERT economics textbook, *Understanding Economic Development*, standard 10, p. 66.

Extract 2.2
Depicting Concepts

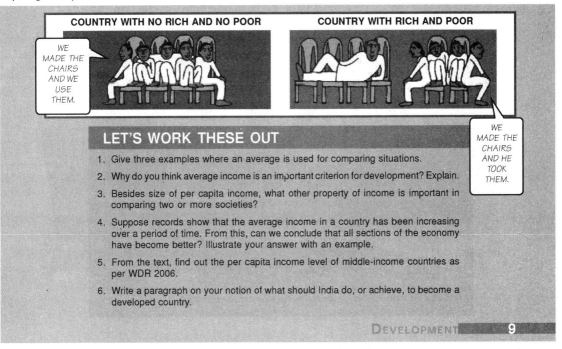

Source: NCERT economics textbook, *Understanding Economic Development*, standard 10, p. 9.

engrossed in digesting a well-chosen illustration. You can ask children to describe the images or write about them. If possible, collect more images that are relevant to the text and use them in class.

69 **Is this also why so many poems and anecdotes are there in the new textbooks?**

Yes, this is the third trick, and probably the most important—the integration of different types of materials. The new textbooks contain extracts from stories, biographies and poems; they also contain fairly extensive narratives of real-life events. In many places there are press reports, news analyses, court orders, archival material, and so on.

Many main principles or concepts of the chapters have been stated directly through these stories and narratives. The stories are not just illustrations (as they were in the earlier textbooks); they embody key concepts (see Extract 2.3). Please keep this in mind when going through the stories and discussing them.

Fig. 6 — The Club of Thinkers, anonymous caricature dating to c. 1820.
The plaque on the left bears the inscription: 'The most important question of today's meeting: How long will thinking be allowed to us?'
The board on the right lists the rules of the Club which include the following:
'1. Silence is the first commandment of this learned society.
2. To avoid the eventuality whereby a member of this club may succumb to the temptation of speech, muzzles will be distributed to members upon entering.'

Source: NCERT history textbook, *India and Contemporary World-II*, standard 9, p. 11.

All these are a break from the earlier style of handling the text because it is important to relate the textbook to the child's real world outside the classroom. Instead of being bookish, such text passages open up a window between the book and the different experiences of the child. They let the child re-think what she sees on television or reads in the newspaper every day (see Extract 2.4).

70 **You mean the narratives and stories are meant to avoid textbooks from feeling textbookish?**

Yes, for example, look at an open-ended question in one of the textbooks (Box 2.4).

What is the answer? Yes and no. Not a simple 'yes' or 'no'. Real life is usually like this—with several factors and complexity. Things were often so simplified in the old textbooks that they seemed to have no connection with real life. Of what use are such textbooks? No wonder that students dismissed

Box 2.4

Do you think that the above is a case of discrimination? Why?

Extract 2.4
Connecting Textbooks with Life

The Right To Know

My dreams have the right to know
Why for centuries they have been
                              breaking
Why don't they ever come true

My hands have the right to know
Why do they remain without work all
                              along
Why do they have nothing to do

My feet have the right to know
Why from village to village they walk
                        on their own
Why are there no signs of a bus yet

My hunger has the right to know
Why grain rots in godowns
While I don't even get a fistful of rice

My old mother has the right to know
Why are there no medicines
Needles, dispensaries or bandages

My children have the right to know
Why do they labour day and night
Why is there no school in sight

What is your favourite line in the above song?

What does the poet mean when he says, "My hunger has the right to know"?

Can you share with your class a local song or a poem on dignity that is from your area?

120 Social and Political Life

Source: NCERT social science textbook, *Social and Political Life-II*, standard 7, p. 120.

school education as textbookish and unrealistic. Remember how the textbooks, in the name of making India more 'democratic', told children what the governments were expected to do (how they *ought to* function). Did that help? The use of realistic examples and narratives is necessary to break out of this trap. It is necessary for the child to learn to negotiate and understand the world around him/her.

71 **Many stories and examples seem complicated and complex. Was that necessary? Why not just give straight and direct definitions for children to learn?**

Real life is complicated, isn't it? It is important that the social sciences get children accustomed to seeing life the way it actually is. If we provide black-and-white or over-simplified pictures to children, we would be doing them a disservice. They would be inadequately prepared to comprehend the world around them (see Extract 2.5). Worse, they might see the world in simplistic, black-and-white terms. This is one reason why we should not shy away from complex and accurate descriptions of social life. There is another reason too.

72 **What is the other reason?**

Definitions that do not relate to concrete situations are difficult to grasp. Their implications and limits are rarely clear.

Extract 2.5
Making Sense of a Complex World

What does TV do to us and what can we do with TV?

In many of our homes, TV is on a lot of the time. In many ways, a lot of our impressions about the world around us are formed by what we see on TV: it is like a 'window on the world'. How do you think it influences us? TV has different types of programmes, soap operas, like *Saas Bhi Kabhi Bahu Thi*, game shows, like *Kaun Banega Crorepati*, reality TV shows like *Big Boss*, news, sports and cartoons. Before, in between and after each programme are advertisements. Since TV time costs so much money, only those programmes that can attract the maximum number of viewers are shown. Can you think of what such programmes might be? Think of what are the kinds of things that TV shows and what it does not. Does it show us more about the lives of the rich or the poor?

We need to think about what TV does to us, how it shapes our views of the world, our beliefs, attitudes and values. We need to realise that it gives us a partial view of the world. While we enjoy our favourite programmes, we should always be aware of the large exciting world beyond our TV screens. There is so much happening out there that TV ignores. A world beyond film stars, celebrities and rich lifestyles, a world that all of us need to reach out to and respond to in various ways. We need to be active viewers, who question whatever we see and hear, while we may enjoy it too!

Source: NCERT social science textbook, *Social and Political Life-II*, standard 7, p. 75.

That is why many good teachers couple the discussion of definitions with a common example from everyday life. The new textbooks assist in that technique. Definitions have been given through discussions of live examples. That helps children visualize the definition much more easily. The concepts get linked with the concrete.

If the student is to only memorize a definition, then the path adopted in the new textbooks seems complex and unnecessary. But if the student is to internalize the definition and be able to use it in evaluating life around herself, then the use of realistic examples is necessary. The new textbooks simplify a teacher's work by providing ready-made examples.

73 There are also lots of boxed sections of text, with borders around them. What is special about them?

We heard some years ago from teachers that they generally leave out all the box items in a textbook. Their approach was 'never waste time on whatever is unimportant at the exams'. A pity!

The boxes highlight certain key aspects of the chapter (see Extract 2.6). In the new textbooks, there are different styles of boxes. For example, in the textbooks, some highlight an extract, others a similar event which took place elsewhere, and yet others contain years and dates. Many boxes contain case studies, brief narratives, and so on. Most of the time, the boxes contain something special and are central to the message of the chapter (see Extract 2.7).

While using the new textbooks, if teachers continue the practice of ignoring boxes, they risk missing important aspects of

Extract 2.6
Framing the Noteworthy: Using Boxes

Grameen Bank of Bangladesh

Grameen Bank of Bangladesh is one of the biggest success stories in reaching the poor to meet their credit needs at reasonable rates. Started in the 1970s as a small project, Grameen Bank now has over 6 million borrowers in about 40,000 villages spread across Bangladesh. Almost all of the borrowers are women and belong to poorest sections of the society. These borrowers have proved that not only are poor women reliable borrowers, but that they can start and run a variety of small income-generating activities successfully.

"If credit can be made available to the poor people on terms and conditions that are appropriate and reasonable these millions of small people with their millions of small pursuits can add up to create the biggest development wonder."

Professor Muhammad Yunus, the founder of Grameen Bank, and recipient of 2006 Nobel Prize for Peace

Source: NCERT economics textbook, *Understanding Economic Development,* standard 10, p. 52.

Jawaharlal Nehru
(1889-1964) born: Uttar
Pradesh. Prime Minister of
the interim government.
Lawyer and Congress
leader. Advocate of
socialism, democracy and
anti-imperialism. Later: First
Prime Minister of India.

Sarojini Naidu
(1879-1949)
born: Andhra Pradesh.
Poet, writer and political
activist. Among the
foremost women leaders in
the Congress. Later:
Governor of Uttar Pradesh.

Somnath Lahiri
(1901-1984) born: West
Bengal. Writer and editor.
Leader of the Communist
Party of India. Later:
Member of West Bengal
Legislative Assembly.

CHECK YOUR PROGRESS

*Long years ago we made a **tryst with destiny**, and now the time comes when we shall redeem our pledge, not wholly or in full measure, but very substantially. At the stroke of the midnight hour, when the world sleeps, India will awake to life and freedom. A moment comes, which comes but rarely in history, when we step out from the old to the new, when an age ends, and when the soul of a nation, long supressed, finds utterance. It is fitting that at this solemn moment we take the pledge of dedication to the service of India and her people and to the still larger cause of humanity ...*

Freedom and power bring responsibility. The responsibility rests upon this Assembly, a sovereign body representing the sovereign people of India. Before the birth of freedom we have endured all the pains of labour and our hearts are heavy with the memory of this sorrow. Some of those pains continue even now. Nevertheless, the past is over and it is the future that beckons to us now.

That future is not one of ease or resting but of incessant striving so that we may fulfil the pledges we have so often taken and the one we shall take today. The service of India means the service of the millions who suffer. It means the ending of poverty and ignorance and disease and inequality of opportunity. The ambition of the greatest man of our generation has been to wipe every tear from every eye. That may be beyond us, but as long as there are tears and suffering, so long our work will not be over.

Read the three quotations above carefully.
- Can you identify one idea that is common to all these three?
- What are the differences in their ways of expressing that common idea?

CONSTITUTIONAL DESIGN   **49**

Source: NCERT political science textbook, *Democratic Politics*, standard 9, p. 49.

Box 2.5

Increasing Students' Interaction and Level of Learning

- **Questions:** Ask students the questions scattered in each chapter. Stimulate discussion. Help them relate the material to what was discussed in another part of the textbook. Make the classroom noisy!

- **Pictures:** Let the students enjoy the cartoons and photographs. Ask them to describe the images. Just as you 'read' text, 'read' the images. Do not skip images, they often speak of the situations in the text. Rarely will you find images of people that would not 'say' anything but give only visual relief to the teacher and the student.

- **Extracts:** Use the extracts from biographies, stories, poems, newspapers to help the student relate to the different forms around him. Social science is closely linked to the everyday world.

a chapter. At times, however, these boxed items mention that you need to read them only if you (teacher or the student) think that the information is important. In such cases, you should use your judgement as to whether you want the students to go through that box or skip it.

74 **But would not all this take a lot of time? How will I finish the course if I am going to have a detailed discussion on every box and picture?**

Yes, you have to manage time well. A good way is to start by keeping a daily diary while you teach the first chapter. At the end of the first chapter (that is, a few days) you will have a feel of how much time is taken up by what. Then, by quickly flipping through a chapter before you teach, you will be able to quickly estimate where you want to let the children loose and where to keep a tight rein. With a little experience, you will soon settle into a new routine.

In some textbooks, the chapters have been written specifically with an eye on the time available. For example, the standard 9 *Democratic Politics* textbook is planned such that each concept or theme gets covered in roughly 15–20 minutes. There could be a small question (or discussion) break before the next section introduces newer things. Usually in classroom situations, teachers handle a subject for 40–45 minutes. Hence, there is enough time for classroom discussions on things happening in society and linking them with the concept learnt.

75 **Wouldn't there be a tendency for the discussions to go on and on, and take up an entire period?**

Yes, there certainly will. And part of the reason for that will be because discussions are much more fun for the teacher too. It is so much nicer to be part of a dialogue than to plod through an elaborate, detailed lecture.

You should be alert about time management for the first few days and work out your own balance. Do not worry, things will fall in place soon. Just keep in mind the magic mantra—children should be learning the basic concepts and that is best done through active learning, not memorization of details (see Box 2.5). Allow the discussion to generate a live feel for the issue and whenever you feel it is beginning to meander, draw the children back to the core issues.

Box 2.6

Conventional Question

Q: What is a democracy?

The traditional way of teaching is to go through the relevant chapter and expect the following answer, copied from page 30.

A: A democracy is a form of government in which (1) rulers elected by the people make all the decisions; (2) elections offer a choice and a fair opportunity to the people to change the current rulers; (3) the choice and opportunity is available to all the people on an equal basis; (4) the exercise of this choice leads to a government limited by basic rules of the constitution and citizens' rights.

Box 2.7

Test the Child's Understanding

Here is some information about four countries. Based on this information, how would you classify each of these countries? Write 'democratic', 'undemocratic' or 'not sure' against each of these:

(a) Country A: People who do not accept the country's official religion do not have a right to vote.

(b) Country B: The same party has been winning elections for the last twenty years.

(c) Country C: Ruling party has lost in the last three elections.

(d) Country D: There is no independent election commission.

Source: NCERT political science textbooks, *Democratic Politics*, standard 9, p. 37.

76 **The questions at the end of each chapter are not straightforward. How do you expect a meaningful evaluation of them?**

The nature of questions was long overdue for change. A straightforward question is very easy to cheat on. By cheating we mean answering it without understanding or learning what was talked about. Let us take an example of a straightforward question which could be asked from the standard 9 *Democratic Politics* textbook (see Box 2.6).

There would be very few who understood the concept (democracy), but most students (and teachers) would memorize the definition, regurgitate it in the examination, remain happy and satisfy others. This is cheating because it maintains appearances, but bypasses the primary purpose—students should understand what is taught.

77 **How else can we ask a question?**

There are several ways. One is by trying to see if the student is able to apply the concepts being taught. In this case, we could ask a question like that given on page 37 of the *Democratic Politics* textbook (see Box 2.7):

To answer this, the student must have gone through the chapter, must be able to recall its basic arguments and must have understood what it is all about. Questions like these are not simple to cheat on. They lead students into learning out of the textbook. A series of such questions can effectively tell us whether or not student has learnt what democracy is.

78 **The questions are too many and bewildering. Earlier there used to be only a few questions, and their answers were simple and easy.**

The questions appear bewildering when you are yet to grasp the basic principles of the chapter. To overcome this difficulty, please go through the chapter carefully and ask yourself 'What are its basic concepts?' In other words, what the chapter tries to convey. Then come back to the questions. You will discover that most questions are merely different ways of asking the same handful of basic issues. The questions are twisted or turned this way or that, and they focus on one aspect or another. But they test basic understanding of a limited range of concepts (see Extract 2.8).

79   Why is this done?

The questions connect the textbook's central concepts and issues with applied and comparative situations. This way, we can ensure that students understand concepts. These exercises also help students to take something from the textbooks which would be useful in their daily lives.

80   It is only while doing the exercises did I begin to understand what the chapter was all about.

Yes, many people have reported such an experience. This happens because your mind began working to connect the chapter's contents with your own life. Earlier, you were only passively reading the chapter. The exercises help students too to understand the chapter better than if we had adopted the usual straightforward questions.

81   Does this mean that I should no longer dictate questions and answers to children?

First, get children to try and figure out the answers by themselves. Then for a few questions, try giving some likely answers. Please make it clear that these are only possible

Extract 2.8
Practising and Consolidating the Grasp of a Basic Concept

10   In 2004 a report published in USA pointed to the increasing inequalities in that country. Inequalities in income reflected in the participation of people in democracy. It also shaped their abilities to influence the decisions taken by the government. The report highlighted that:
- If an average Black family earns $ 100 then the income of average White family is $ 162. A White family has twelve times more wealth than the average Black family.
- In a President's election 'nearly nine out of 10 individuals in families with income over $ 75,000 have voted. These people are the top 20 % of the population in terms of their income. On the other hand only 5 people out of 10 from families with income less than $ 15,000 have voted. They are the bottom 20% of the population in terms of their income.
- About 95 % contribution to the political parties comes from the rich. This gives them opportunity to express their opinion and concern, which is not available to most citizens.
- As poor sections participate less in politics, the government does not listen to their concerns – coming out of poverty, getting job, education, health care and housing form them. Politicians hear most regularly about the concerns of business and the most rich.
Write an essay on 'Democracy and Poverty' using the information given in this report but using examples from India.

Source: NCERT political science textbook, *Democratic Politics*, standard 9, p. 39.

Box 2.8

How to Encourage Children to Think on Their Own

Pick up two or three excellent answers from the children's responses, and present them as examples of what is desired. Teachers who have done so said that this encouraged the children to think on their own. You can thus avoid the closing finality of your own answer.

answers, not model answers. Otherwise, children might repeat your answers in their answer books.

Encourage children to write answers in their own language and style. Do not expect or insist that every child should answer in a similar manner (see Box 2.8). If you insist, you will not find out whether the child has learnt. Insisting on the same or very similar answer will also hinder the growth of the child's own understanding and imagination (see Box 2.9).

Box 2.9

Role Reversal

Dear teacher, we've got a question for you. For essay-type answers, how do you give marks to the students?
Teacher: I count the number of 'points' in the model answer, verify whether the student has mentioned the 'points' and give marks.

If you look only for 'points', it means that you expect only memorization. It is essential to enable children to develop their own answers.
What do you mean?

Let children write their own answers. Let them develop their language skills. Look for conceptual understanding, not points.
But then, they will make mistakes.

If they make mistakes, that is fine. Tell them where they have gone wrong. Do you give feedback to the students?
At times, I write 'good', 'excellent', etc.

Do you think that helps the students?
Well, I am not sure.

When you evaluate, please write detailed suggestions on how the child could have improved the answer.
That is time-consuming.

Yes, but that is what helps the child. You could also write:
1. **'Liked the way the ideas are organized.'**
2. **'The new examples you have given are apt.'**
Oh! Ok, I understand.

Similarly, for answers to be improved, you could add:
1. **How the ideas can be better organized**
2. **What important issues he missed**
   (a) **'The link between the two concepts is unclear.'**
   (b) **'The examples did not lead to your conclusion.'**
3. **'If your answer had developed on the following lines, I would have given you more marks.'**

Box 2.10

A Teacher Reports

'Since it is interesting for the teacher too, my life and work have become much less frustrating and boring. Less dictation of questions and answers!'

Source: Teacher interviewed by Amman Madan, Kanpur, 2007.

82 **Would this mean too much work for us teachers?**

Not really. Once you shift to this style of teaching, it is just as much work as the previous style. Those of us who do it have found that it is no more effort than a mechanical style of giving feedback.

Yes, the teacher will have to stay more alert in class. Checking of answer books also slows down, because you no longer merely 'tick' the same answer in every answer book. But the boost you give to a child's growth more than balances the effort you put in. For many of us, the greatest payback is the enhanced pleasure of interacting with students in the classroom; the approach to questions and evaluations in the new textbooks leads to greater job satisfaction (see Box 2.10).

83 **Textbooks have changed. Will the examination pattern too change? Are we expected to make new sets of questions for evaluating children?**

Board exams are expected to change, and follow the pattern set by the new NCERT textbooks. So it would be good if you changed the various class exams to the new pattern.

84 **Has there been any serious effort in the past to change the examination system in India?**

There have been efforts to reform examination systems, but only a few. Kerala has by and large given up the ranking system and moved to a grading system. The Madhya Pradesh government partnered with Eklavya to conduct a board exam at standard 8—it was an open book exam, and tested students' understanding (rather than memory). They used a mix of questions to examine children's comprehension and ability to apply concepts. Every year they prepared a new set of questions, none of which was the same as those in the textbooks.

Indian education systems were designed to distinguish between 'successful' and 'failed' students; the examinations themselves were not seen as constructive tools. Nowadays, the NCERT and the Central Board of Secondary Education (CBSE) favour rethinking the basic pattern of examinations.

85 **With the new textbooks, what will question papers look like? What will be the pattern of examinations?**

It is too early to say what the exam pattern will be. But most likely, the questions will test a variety of skills. While designing questions in the textbooks, the writers took care to tap various skills considered necessary for developing in children. To make that effort meaningful, the question papers too should reflect this approach and maintain the diversity of questions.

Teachers will have to come up with new question papers of their own. While doing so, please remember to think beyond the old-type, descriptive questions (what, where, which). Preparation of new question papers can be undertaken at a district level initially, in a group, if teachers find it convenient.

86 How can teachers, on their own, make questions for tests and examinations?

Let us begin with how *not* to ask questions.

Avoid straightforward questions that test only memorization of details. Instead, ask questions that call for applying a concept the child may have learnt. For example, in history for standard 6, the chapter 'On the Trail of the Earliest People' discusses the life of early humans in India.

Look at the two types of questions that can be asked (see Box 2.11):

The old-type question is easy to evaluate (check the number of sites listed by the child and assign marks), but is a bad question. Children can cram names (Bhimbetka, Inamgaon, Paliyapalli) but still remain without a feel for the early lives of humans in India. Look at the new-type questions. They direct the children to an important historical issue— the factors which guided human habitation in the early centuries. The factors and their interplay deepen children's understanding. Also, from the child's angle, it would be more interesting to learn how different or similar life was in the past, than a mere list of names.

87 Should we ask such analytical or applied questions everywhere?

No. There should also be a few questions which examine whether the child has her facts correct, or can talk about the concepts in a systematic way. Only a few questions of this type are necessary, though.

88 What other kinds of questions can there be?

If you look carefully at the exercises at the end of each chapter in a textbook, you will notice different kinds of questions.

Box 2.11

Old-type Questions

Q. At what sites have remains of early humans been found in India?

Q. Where did early humans choose to live?

New-type Questions

Q. At what kinds of sites have remains of early humans been found in India?

Q. If you were part of an early human community in India, how would you choose where to live?

Box 2.12

Comparative

3. What differences do you find between private and public health services in your area? Use the following table to compare and contrast these.

Facility	Cost of services	Availability of service
Private		
Public		

Source: NCERT social science textbook, *Social and Political Life II*, standard 7, p. 29.

Box 2.13

Extrapolative

Q. Do you think merchants and bankers today have the kind of influence they had in the eighteenth century?

Q. Did any of the kingdoms mentioned in this chapter develop in your state? If so, in what ways do you think life in the state would have been different in the eighteenth century from what it is in the twenty-first century?

Source: NCERT history textbook, *Our Pasts II*, standard 7, p. 90, p. 154.

Please look at the question in Box 2.12 which appears at the end of a chapter on state governments. Box 2.13 has examples from the history textbook of standard 7.

Flip through the new textbooks for other types of questions; there are many possibilities once you decide not to ask plain vanilla, memorization questions.

Please remember to ask questions which the classroom experience has prepared the child for. All questions need not have been discussed in the classroom, but the type of question must be one that the child is familiar with. Your exam questions should challenge the child to think a little deeper, but must also be one that the child can realistically answer. Avoid asking over-complicated questions which may be beyond a child's understanding. You know your students well!

89 **The chapters are full of too many details. The children have to mug up all these irrelevant facts. You have made our students' lives hell.**

Please do not look at the new textbooks with old lenses. Students are *not* expected to memorize all the details in the chapters. The details are given (as examples) to help the children think and learn the concepts.

90 **How do so many details help the child learn concepts?**

Let us take an example. Please read the following extract from the first chapter of the standard 9 *Democratic Politics* textbook (see Box 2.14).

Now, there are all kinds of details here—the date of the strike, the name of the shipyard, the pronunciation of Lech Walesa and so on. But there is no need for children to memorize all these, or for questions to be asked about them. These are only concrete details provided to let children get a feel of reality. What is important is that democracy means the freedom to form an independent association as well as freedom of speech.

Now, how will we ask questions in an exam? (see Box 2.15)

The old-type question is bad because it does not tell us whether the student learnt anything important. The new-type question is better because it tests whether the

Box 2.14

On 14 August 1980, the workers of Lenin Shipyard in the city of Gdansk went on a **strike**. The shipyard was owned by the government. In fact all the factories and big property in Poland were owned by the government. The strike began with a demand to take back a crane operator, a woman worker, who was unjustly dismissed from service. This strike was illegal, because **trade unions** independent of the ruling party were not allowed in Poland. As the strike continued, a former electrician of the shipyard, Lech Walesa (pronounced Lek Walesha), joined the strikers. He was dismissed from service in 1976 for demanding higher pay. Walesa soon emerged as the leader of the striking workers. The strike began to spread across the whole city. Now the workers started raising larger demands. They wanted the right to form independent trade unions. They also demanded the release of **political prisoners** and an end to censorship on press.

Source: NCERT political science textbook, *Democratic Politics*, pp. 5–6.

Box 2.15

Old-type question

Q. Which strike started off Lech Walesa's movement?

New-type question

Q. Poland at the time of Lech Walesa's great strike claimed to be a democracy. Would you agree with that claim?

Extract 2.9
Unforgettable Lessons

Activity

The year is 1921. You are a student in a government-controlled school. Design a poster urging school students to answer Gandhiji's call to join the Non-Cooperation Movement.

Source: NCERT history textbook, *India and Contemporary World-II*, standard 10, p. 58.

Box 2.16

Confucian Maxim

What I hear, I forget

What I see, I remember

What I do, I understand.

student has understood some of the basic principles (or key features) of a democracy. The new-type question also draws the student's attention to the flaws in a government's claim.

91 **That is a relief. Life becomes easier for students with such an approach.**

Yes and no. A boring and meaningless part of life is struck away—a student no longer needs to remember many pointless details. On the other hand, we now expect that she will use her mind much more than in the past. We hope that the new approach towards education will create brighter and better human beings.

Activities and Projects

92 **The new textbooks have lots of 'activities'. Do you really think we will have time to do all of them?**

A core principle of the new approach to education (across all subjects) is the emphasis on activities (see Extract 2.9). All educationists would agree that when children do things by themselves, it improves their various skills. This idea is rooted in the wise saying, usually attributed to Confucius (see Box 2.16).

93 Many students get the 'activities' done through shops. How can we curb that?

We have heard that 'activities' in the textbooks are converted into 'projects' for high-school students, who are required to do a few projects every year. To curb this, teachers and parents should act.

Teachers should assign activities that are achievable, and those that do not call for parents to rush to the market late at night to buy raw materials. Once the activities are practical and doable, then parents will have less need to rely on a shop that 'sells' ready-made project kits. Parents should also realize (and be made to realize by teachers) that children benefit from doing the activities. Children, not parents or shopkeepers, should undertake the activity (see Extract 2.10). Only then will the purpose of activities be fulfilled.

Experiences of Textbook Changes Across the Country

94 A drastic change in textbooks seems to have happened for the first time. Have such textbooks been used by teachers anywhere in India?

It has long been known that traditional Indian textbooks communicate poorly with children. Despite national reports and committees on educational reform talking about this, there was never a national-level decision or effort to make the content accessible to children. But in the last 20 years or so, there were some major initiatives in state-level textbooks. The new NCERT textbooks are latecomers, in that sense.

In the 1980s, the NGO Eklavya, produced innovative textbooks for use in primary and middle schools in Madhya Pradesh. In the 1990s, there were serious attempts to improve the textbooks in Rajasthan, Chhattisgarh, Assam, Delhi and Kerala. Many of these efforts were part of larger changes under schemes like the District Primary Education Programme (DPEP) and Lok Jumbish. These radical changes in state-level textbooks were mostly limited to middle schools,

A wallpaper project

A wallpaper is an interesting activity through which research can be done on particular topics of interest. The following photographs explain the different aspects involved in creating a wallpaper in a classroom.

Find out with the help of your teacher, the work done by the government departments mentioned above, and fill in the table.

After introducing the topic and having a brief discussion with the whole class, the teacher divides the class into groups. The group discusses the issue and decides what it would like to include in the wall-paper. Children then work individually or in pairs to read the collected material and write their observations or experiences. They can do this through creating stories, poems, case studies, interviews, etc.

The group looks at the material that they have selected, drawn or written. They read each other's writing and provide feedback to each other. They make decisions on what should be included and finalise the layout for the wallpaper.

Source: NCERT social science textbook, *Social and Political Life-II*, standard 7, p. 39.

except in Kerala, where there were changes all the way up to the board examinations in standard 10. In Kerala, when students finish high school, they are given grades, not marks.

Question 13

The innovative state-level textbooks of that period had a close affinity with the National Curriculum Framework (NCF) of 1986.

95 **How did teachers in these states respond to the changes? Did they feel that their workload had increased?**

Initially the teachers complained that the workload had increased. This was natural—the textbooks were new after all. The teachers also had to think of ways to use the textbooks in classrooms. So, there was an increase in workload. But after a year or two, when teachers became familiar and experienced with the new nature of work, 'increased workload' was no longer a major difficulty.

A few months into using the new textbooks, almost all teachers said that the new books were more accessible to the students. They later reported better learning and improved understanding among students.

The new national-level textbooks of the NCERT draw a lot from the efforts, experiences and lessons of various states.

Teachers' Ability to Teach the New Textbooks

96 **Your suggestions and ideas sound quite useful. But frankly, it is only when I try them out will I really know how good (or bad) they are. Where can I learn more about how to use books like these?**

At the beginning of each new textbook is a note to the teacher on how the textbook has been re-designed, what new features have been included in the textbook, and so on. There are also specific suggestions on how to teach that textbook. In most textbooks, each chapter has an overview or introduction, which summarizes the key elements discussed in that chapter. Please use that to organize your understanding of the chapter.

In addition, you will the find the following useful:

1. *Divaswapna* by Gijubhai—Published by the National Book Trust and available for Rs 25, the book gives lots

of ideas (with examples) on how to teach well in India. Not all of his experiments can probably be tried in your school (especially if your principal is not sympathetic to Gijubhai's approach!) but it will give you several ideas to insert in your work.

2. *http://www.arvindguptatoys.com*—A compendium of excellent writings on education and teaching. Also lots of toys which children can make and play with, and take apart to learn their underlying principles.

3. *http://www.vidyaonline.net*—A heap of good resources for primary- and middle-school teachers.

4. *http://www.eledu.net*—Get ideas and advice from experts and colleagues. Resources and online discussions from the University–School Resource Network.

97 How can teachers provide feedback to those who prepare textbooks?

You can write to any or all of the following:

1. *The department in the NCERT that prepared the textbook*— Every book contains the official address of the NCERT and the name of the department which prepared that textbook;

2. *Chief Advisor or Member–Coordinator of the Textbook Development Committee of that textbook*—They are subject experts who participated in preparing the books and their names appear in the textbook. They may or may not reply, but they will definitely read and think about what you write to them;

3. *E-mail contacts*—Some textbooks mention the e-mail address to which teachers and students can send comments. For example, it is *politics.ncert@gmail.com* in the standard 9 textbook *Democratic Politics* and *spl_ncert@hotmail.com* in the *Social and Political Life* textbooks for standard 6 to 8. Many comments have been received at these e-mail addresses.

Responses from teachers and students are important and valuable. All responses are filed. They will influence revisions and changes in textbooks in the future.

Supplementary Materials for Teachers

98 **Can I use textbooks from other publishers for teaching my subject?**

The CBSE has made it mandatory for secondary schools to use the new NCERT textbooks in standards 9 and 10. To update their own knowledge base, teachers can use non-NCERT books and other information sources. Teachers will benefit from different kinds of resources:

1. Journals for teachers like *Sandarbh* (Hindi, Marathi and Gujarati), *Shiksha Vimarsh* (Hindi), *Tulir* (Tamil) and *Teacher Plus* (English). These contain articles aimed at enlarging teachers' understanding of the topics taught in school.

2. Good B.A. level course material, such as those published by the Indira Gandhi National Open University. These help teachers keep track of recent advancements in a subject. Also, teachers who feel that they studied an old curriculum at the university level, will benefit from such material.

3. 'Readers' in social sciences used by B.A. and M.A. teachers. For example, in political science, Oxford University Press publishes the series *Themes in Indian Politics*, and SAGE Publications brings out the series *Readings in Indian Government and Politics*. These collections of classic articles help teachers identify the best learning material for deepening their own understanding of a subject. Newspaper supplements for children. Teachers can use these directly in classrooms. Children will enjoy reading them. These days, English and regional language newspapers carry supplements for children. Some newspapers also run Newspaper-in-Education programmes that teachers can collaborate on.

99 **Can you give some examples of books that can be used by students for supplementary reading?**

Any book which you feel that a student can read and understand by herself can be used for supplementary reading. These can be kept in your school's library.

Sadly, social science books targeted at teenage readers are rare in India. For middle-school students, Eklavya has developed illustrated (yet inexpensive) booklets on many themes discussed in the new textbooks. On Indian history, there are a few publications from Tulika and Puffin Books. The National Book Trust has several readable books aimed at a general audience; these can be used by younger readers. On issues directly relating to environment, the *Down to Earth* magazine's supplement 'Gobar Times' is a good resource. *Balarama Digest* (editions in English and Malayalam) sometimes covers social science issues in interesting ways.

Chapter 3

STUDENTS

Learning from the New Textbooks

100 **My teacher gives me answers ('notes') to the questions in the textbook. She says, 'This is what you should write in the exam.'**

When the old textbooks were used, questions in the textbook were often asked in the examination too. But when the new textbooks are used, the questions in the examination may not be the same as the questions in the textbooks. To do well in the examination, you should learn and understand the ideas in the chapter, instead of learning the answer to specific questions.

The new textbooks encourage you to think on your own. Write your own answers, not the 'notes' given by teachers. Please practise writing the answers by yourself (instead of memorizing the teacher's answers) to do well in the examination.

101 **I like cartoons. Why not make the whole textbook in comic format?**

Yes, cartoons are interesting. But can we express everything in cartoons? Can you write the entire examination as a comic sheet? It will take a long time to convey an idea, no? So, some ideas are conveyed by cartoons, but not all.

Think of your friend who likes text-based descriptions—poems, novels, and stories—and finds text easy to learn. She would not like a comic book. To make her learning enjoyable, we use examples that are not cartoons.

Some complain that children are not mature enough to understand cartoons. They fear that children might see everything as a joke, instead of respecting the ideals or recognizing the importance of an idea. For example, in a chapter on

Box 3.1

Write Back

Send your comments, ideas, criticisms to the NCERT. They do make a difference! See Question 97 for details.

elections, a cartoon portrays voters as dogs, and politicians' promises as food (see Extract 3.1). Some complained that the cartoon does not correctly convey the idea of politicians representing the people.

102 How can I help in the design of better textbooks for us?

Tell the NCERT what you think about a cartoon, a boxed item, the text, or anything. Your feedback will help it improve the textbooks (see Box 3.1). Are the letters too small or big? Are the sentences difficult for you to understand? Please give examples when you write to them.

If necessary, please seek the help of your parents or teachers, to find a postal or e-mail address.

Examinations and Careers

103 Can those who study and use social sciences, earn as much as those who study science, engineering or medicine?

In a country, specialists are needed in all fields. So, there are well-paying jobs in many fields, including those that involve little physics, engineering or medicine. These days, MBAs earn well and many of them studied social sciences in college. The MBA course itself contains social subjects like economics, politics and human relations. There are also other professionals like lawyers, journalists and researchers who studied social sciences (and apply their learning) and earn well when they work in government, firms or non-governmental organizations.

104 In competitive exams, for jobs and good courses in India, the emphasis is still on facts and information. So, when you say that the emphasis should be on understanding of issues (rather than memorizing facts), you are 'weakening' me.

Learning to think is an asset; it does not reduce your ability to memorize facts. The new textbooks do not ask you to ignore the facts. They help you dig out facts, and analyse what the facts mean.

There are different kinds of competitive exams in India. The civil services exam largely tests your memory. But to do well in them and also in more sophisticated entrance exams for courses such as MBA or social work or journalism courses, you cannot succeed with merely memorizing—these test your understanding and intelligence, and you need to learn to think through situations.

In any case, none of the competitive exams will remain the same for ever. It is smarter, therefore, to learn various skills instead of merely preparing for a particular examination that you might write immediately after school or college.

Again, please do not think that all objective-type questions (a popular form in competitive exams) test only memory. Look at the example in Box 3.2.

If you can answer that question, it does not mean that you will be handicapped in tackling a traditional, memory-based, objective-type questions like the one in Box 3.3.

Question 2

Box 3.2

Consider the following two statements on power sharing and select the answer using the codes given below:

(A) Power sharing is good for democracy.

(B) It helps to reduce the possibility of conflict between social groups.

Which of these statements is true?

a. A is true but B is false;

b. Both A and B are true;

c. Both A and B are false;

d. A is false but B is true.

Box 3.3

Many of the campaigns in northern India were fought over the city of _____. (Tanjore, Nasik, Kanauj)

In a short period of _____ years Mahmud made _____ raids. (five, ten, fifteen, twenty-five, ten, twelve, seventeen, eighteen)

Integration of Social Sciences

105 **Why do the four textbooks in social sciences teach the subjects in different styles?**

Those who write textbooks come from various backgrounds—some are teachers but they teach at different levels (school, college, university), others are educationists and trainers of teachers, and still others have expertise in the subject but not in education. This makes it difficult to achieve common standards on how to design textbooks or how to best convey concepts to children. Moreover, the Indian education system has till now focused on producing only one type of professionals—teachers. There are no institutions to train people who wish to be professional curriculum designers or education managers or educational policymakers or education officers. That too hinders the development of good, common standards.

Also, more than Indian political scientists or economists, Indian historians have creatively thought about the school textbooks in their subject; the new textbooks in history are therefore more innovative than the other social science textbooks. This has happened probably because history textbooks have been in the limelight repeatedly in India, with politicians and the public joining the debates in the media. History teaching has thus attracted interest, and subject specialists have felt the need to keep the subject alive and interesting for students. The specialists in other social sciences are yet to put in sufficient efforts into school textbooks.

Pedagogic Approach/Examinations

106 **These books look so different from the older ones. I am expected to do so much more in them!**

Yes, one big difference is that the new textbooks expect students to do and learn. The books are designed to encourage active learning. Sitting quietly and listening to your teachers helps to maintain order and discipline, but leads to slow learning. You will learn much more if you do things, think about issues, get excited about pictures, or 'feel' a story. Be alive in the classroom!

107 **Cool! That means I no longer need to sit quietly; I can freely make a racket and shout in class.**

That was not what we meant. To learn actively, there should also be some coordination and dialogue in the classroom. Too much activity in the class does not help learning. You would not hear the teacher, he would not hear you, and the principal will come and yell at all of you!

Yes, speak up in the classroom. If there is a picture you like, say so; if there is something you do not understand, ask about it; when asked a question, if you have something to say (even if it is not the complete answer), tell the class. Be active—that is the best way to learn.

 *Question 62*

108 **There are lots of pictures and cartoons in the new textbooks. Did you put them there just to make us laugh?**

You are smart. There is more to the illustrations than making students smile. The illustrations and cartoons say something important to you. What they say is usually one of the

Question 68 basic issues discussed in that chapter. Along with enjoying the illustration (and cackling in mirth), please try to guess what that picture is trying to say (see Extract 3.1).

109 There are so many questions in some of the new textbooks. Are we supposed to mug up all the answers to these questions?

The good news is that you no longer need to 'mug up' the answers to questions. What you need to figure out are the basic concepts of each chapter. Once you can understand and apply those, then you will be able to answer all the questions without any 'mugging'.

Extract 3.1
Not Just for Laughs

So if a political party is motivated only by desire to be in power, even then it will be forced to serve the people. This is a bit like the way market works. Even if a shopkeeper is interested only in his profit, he is forced to give good service to the customers. If he does not, the customer will go to some other shop. Similarly, political competition may cause divisions and some ugliness, but it finally helps to force political parties and leaders to serve the people.

Read these two cartoons carefully. Write the message of each of them in your own words. Have a discussion in class on which of the two is closer to the reality in your own locality. Draw a cartoon to depict what elections do to the relationship between voters and political leaders.

Source: NCERT political science textbook, *Democratic Politics*, standard 9, p. 60.

Why do girls like to go to school together in groups?

Source: NCERT social science textbook, *Social and Political Life-II*, standard 7, p. 45.

Question 89

There are many questions because your mind needs exercise. When you have gone through all the exercises and questions, you will have a good and deep understanding. You will be able to tackle real-life situations and perhaps even have a better life.

110 **You mean, I do not even need to remember all those details of names and places given in the stories and examples?**

Yes, there is no need to remember every detail. The textbooks have lots of examples in the form of stories, boxes, and so on. These are only examples, and are meant to help you understand. Instead of cramming all the details, you should try to understand the basic concepts and the basic processes at work. You should then apply that understanding while looking at the world around you.

Of course, there are some important facts and details you should know, for instance, that India has a parliament. But do not waste your time memorizing what happened in Chilean politics 30 years ago!

111 **There seem to be no single, correct answers to many questions in the new textbooks. I find the subject confusing.**

Take the question from the chapter on Gender in the standard 7 textbook *Social and Political Life* (see Extract 3.2).

There can be several answers to it: 'because they feel safer while walking in groups in public spaces', 'because they are more socially oriented while growing up in the family', and so on. What is important is not narrowing down to one, single answer. What is important is to draw your attention to a facet of life which you may not have noticed, and to get you to think about its implications. Why do girls feel more vulnerable? Why and how do they learn to be more social?

Just as there are several answers to the same question, it is possible to say the same thing in several ways—the words and examples used differ from one student to another. What is the need for all students to write the same, common, 'mugged up' answer?

Question 76

Chapter 4

EDUCATIONISTS

112 **What are the salient features of the new textbooks? How are they different from the older ones?**

Most importantly, across all three subjects—history, political science and economics—there has been an effort to move away from the conventional style of giving definitions and information. The new textbooks try to avoid listings of events, jargon, images which are mere fillers, and questions that promote only rote learning. They invite children to learn and draw conclusions from examples, narratives, case studies, sources, images and cartoons. In the design and presentation of textbooks, much has been achieved (see Extracts 4.1 and 4.2). And there has been some degree of success in making the text itself friendly to the child reader. The role of the teacher is expected to move away from that of a knowledge repository to that of a facilitator in the child's learning process. Questions and discussions (for use in the classroom) require the child to not just remember facts and figures, but also acquire a fairly deep understanding, or at least recognition, of the complexities of the themes.

Question 58

113 **What are the major deficiencies of the new textbooks?**

1. Different subjects have pitched their content and language at different levels. Some textbooks are more readable (child-friendly) than others.

2. Similarly, there is considerable (avoidable) variation in the styles, and quality of images and photographs used.

3. Questions and methods used in the textbooks have not been standardized.

were also the *bhakti* saints. They had a longer history in India. The *alvars* and the *nayannars* of the Tamil devotional cult had started the tradition of preaching the idea of *bhakti* through hymns and stories. This movement had been popular with the merchants and artisans in the towns and the peasants in the villages. The *bhakti* movement continued the same teaching. Most of the saints were from the non-brahmin castes. The *bhakti* teachers also taught that the relationship between man and God was based on love, and worshipping God with devotion was better than merely performing any number of religious ceremonies. They stressed the need for tolerance among men and religions.

Chaitanya was a religious teacher who preached in Bengal. He became a devotee of Krishna and composed many hymns to Krishna. He would gather together a group of people to whom he preached and to whom he taught the hymns. He travelled in various parts of the country and then settled at Puri, in Orissa. In Maharashtra, *bhakti* was preached by Jnaneshvara. He also rewrote the *Gita* in Marathi so that the ordinary people who had not been educated in Sanskrit could understand the *Gita*. Even more popular were Namadeva and in a later period Tukaram, both of whom continued to preach the idea of devotion to God through love.

In Banaras there was a weaver called Kabir who was also a *bhakti* saint. The *dohas* or couplets which Kabir composed and taught to his followers are still recited. Kabir tried to make a bridge between Hinduism and Islam. He felt that religious differences do not matter, for what really matters is that everyone should love God. God has many names, Some call him Rama, others Rahim. Some call him Hari, others Allah. So why should people fight over the name of God. The followers of Kabir formed a separate group known as *Kabirpanthis*. At a later period Surdas and Dau continued the *bhakti* tradition.

There was another religious teacher who was as important as Kabir and whose followers some centuries later became very powerful in northern India. This was Nanak who founded the Sikh religion. According to the Sikh tradition, Nanak was the son of a village accountant and lived in the Punjab. Nanak's brother-in-law helped him to get employment in the office of the local governor, Daulat Khan Lodi, but Nanak's heart was not in his work. So he left his job and travelled all over the country. Guru Nanak finally returned and settled down at Kartarpur now called Dera Baba Nanak. His teachings in the form of verses are included in a scripture called the *Adi Granth* which was compiled by his fourth successor in the early 17th century. Nanak taught

Source: From NCERT social science textbook, *Social Sciences*, standard 7, 2005, p. 51.
Note: Differences in textbooks: Nayanars and Alwars are presented in the new textbook of history (facing page) with more elements and colour than in the old textbook (above).

Hagiography
Writing of saints'
lives.

Nayanars and Alvars

There were 63 Nayanars, who belonged to different caste backgrounds such as potters, "untouchable" workers, peasants, hunters, soldiers, Brahmanas and chiefs. The best known among them were Appar, Sambandar, Sundarar and Manikkavasagar. There are two sets of compilations of their songs – *Tevaram* and *Tiruvacakam*.

There were 12 Alvars, who came from equally divergent backgrounds, the best known being Periyalvar, his daughter Andal, Tondaradippodi Alvar and Nammalvar. Their songs were compiled in the *Divya Prabandham*.

Fig. 2
A bronze image of
Manikkavasagar.

Between the tenth and twelfth centuries the Chola and Pandya kings built elaborate temples around many of the shrines visited by the saint-poets, strengthening the links between the bhakti tradition and temple worship. This was also the time when their poems were compiled. Besides, **hagiographies** or religious biographies of the Alvars and Nayanars were also composed. Today we use these texts as sources for writing histories of the bhakti tradition.

The devotee and the Lord

This is a composition of Manikkavasagar:

Into my vile body of flesh
You came, as though it were a temple of gold,
And soothed me wholly and saved me,
O Lord of Grace, O Gem most Pure,
Sorrow and birth and death and illusion
You took from me, and set me free.
O Bliss! O Light! I have taken refuge in You,
And never can I be parted from You.

? *How does the poet describe his relationship with the deity?*

OUR PASTS – II   106

Source: NCERT history textbook, *Our Parts-II*, standard 7, p. 106.

Box 4.1

Exams vs Education

So often, in the name of 'objectivity', teachers sacrifice flexibility and creativity. Very often teachers, in government as well as private schools, insist that all children must give identical answers to questions. The argument given for not accepting other answers is that, "They cannot give answers that are not there in the textbook." "We discussed it in the staffroom and decided that we will only accept this answer is right!", or that "There will be too many types of answers. Then should we accept them all?" Such arguments make a travesty of the meaning of learning and only serve to convince children and parents that schools are irrationally rigid. We must ask ourselves why we only ask children to *give answers* to questions. Even the ability to make a set of questions for given answers is a valid test of learning.

Source: Excerpted from the National Curriculum Framework, 2005.

Question 76

4. Not every textbook has been able to make the linkage between its content and the social context within which children live.

5. References to materials outside the textbook are still inadequate.

6. Much more needs to be done in providing clear guidelines and examples to the teachers, on how to use these textbooks.

7. Textbook planning (especially in terms of the content across subjects) remains patchy.

114 With such fundamental changes in textbooks, will there be a change in the pattern of examinations?

Educationists have long been debating how to evaluate children and even whether to evaluate. The present National Curriculum Framework (NCF) has a strong and clear position on the need to rethink examinations (see Box 4.1).

While discussing with teachers we observed that one of their main concerns was the examination—that is, how to handle the wide variety of questions in the new textbooks, at the time of examination. The new textbooks have introduced some new ways of posing questions. If it leads to a new approach towards evaluation and a change in the pattern of examinations, that would be good.

In India, we have two extreme models of examination questions: questions for long essay-type answers (popular at the university level, and where questions generally begin with *what, when, where* or *how*), and quiz-type objective questions. These models test how good you are at filling pages, or memorizing information. They do not tell us whether children have actually learned what has been taught in the textbooks or what the teacher has tried to teach. Have the students internalized the knowledge and are they able to use it in real life? Probably, the answer lies in a middle path that assesses the real learning outcomes. The questions in the new textbooks try to adopt a new approach, but there are variations across the new textbooks. This has happened despite the early recognition that designing questions was a distinct and huge task in the making of the new textbooks.

115 **You seem to be going all the way against information-based textbooks. Isn't that a bias, and one which is equally dangerous?**

One reason why information was thought essential was that we need information to defend an argument that we wish to make. But while emphasizing information, we forgot that we also need to inculcate how to consider or build an argument. For instance, how does one systematically read, analyse and understand a passage from which information can be gathered? Children were always tested on their ability to recall the information, rather than their ability to build an argument or evaluate a situation.

The new textbooks do not throw out information altogether. In many of the new textbooks, information has been integrated into certain contexts. We see information as part of a comprehensive and deeper approach towards human knowledge.

116 **Talking of information-based textbooks and examination patterns, I feel that Indian education has been infected by 'guides'—books tailored for a student to succeed in examinations. This is a failure of textbooks, which were neither child-friendly nor exam-friendly. Will this situation change?**

Education in India has become the celebration of examinations, particularly school-leaving examinations ('board exams'). 'Guides' became popular because textbooks did not address the children directly, and the examination system became predictable. A textbook should explain the content in a direct and simple manner to develop the child's understanding. Most old textbooks made concepts appear complex, and students found guide books easier to read. Similarly, exams should test a child's knowledge and whether she has understood the material to be learnt. By asking direct questions and expecting direct answers, exams were poorly designed and predictable, so much so that guide books with 'model' answers were the best bet for a child who wanted to clear an exam.

It is too early to say whether the new textbooks will drive away guide books. Based on feedback, the textbooks themselves need to be made simpler in the years ahead. Using the new textbook's approach to questions, examinations could be made less predictable. Till then, guides are here

Box 4.2

Geography Teaching-learning

If geography currently languishes as a social study, the reasons lie within its own nature of discourse characterized by frameworks of physical-human dualism and a positivistic and deterministic approach. A review of teaching-learning materials shows that such practices in geography hinder appreciation of socio-spatial implications. Recent geographies have marked major shifts from the traditional framework by engaging in understandings of socio-spatial transformations. But our educational practices continue to operate within traditional limitations.

Source: Yemuna Sunny, 2006. 'Analysing Current Practices in Geography Education'. *Economic and Political Weekly* 41(3): pp. 270–278.

to stay. After all, a new approach to learning, teaching and evaluation takes time to evolve.

Need to Rethink Social Science Curriculum

117 Children are taught Indian history in middle school and world history in high school. Why? How does one prioritize the concepts that are taught across various classes?

In India, the tradition has been to teach history in this sequence. Perhaps those who wrote the early textbooks considered India close (or immediately known) to the child, and the 'world' to be away. The child can learn about the world after studying events in one's own country.

118 If so, when the child is learning India in history, why is he learning the 'universe' in geography?

Again, this has been handed down in the teaching system. Senior academics did not explore seriously whether this would help the children or their learning processes. The geographers would have thought that for the child to understand why there are different climates in a region like India, she has to first know the universe. When they write textbooks, geographers often refer to India as a whole; this does not help the children understand regional variations (see Box 4.2). Unlike the geographer who tries to build upon a broad perspective, the historian tries to first present the child's immediate surroundings. Many state-level history textbooks try to build upon the history of their respective states.

119 You mean to say that sufficient thought did not go into the designing of social science textbooks in India?

Mental rigidities exist. Some believe that changing the order of teaching will kill their subjects. They fear to think differently. They ask, 'After all, we learned it that way. Is it not okay to teach our children too in the same way?' In such a situation, we miss opportunities to provide alternative ways of thinking. Probably if I had been taught differently I would have become different.

The new NCERT textbooks try to loosen such rigidities, at least in some subjects. One important innovation in them is the emphasis on methods. For example, the new history textbooks emphasize how a historian goes about her work. Textbooks are laid out in a certain chronological order, but at each level, children are expected to do what a historian does—examine various sources and try to validate what could be a correct interpretation of that particular period of history.

Question 133

A Better Method of Teaching

120 **Where there is no unanimity in deciding the content, surely there will be no unanimity in the method of teaching either. An idea can be taught in various ways.**

Hmm…let us take an example. Imagine that you want to teach how the government gets formed. What will be a good way to teach this? In our old way of teaching social sciences, we give a definition like, 'In a democracy, government is formed by adult franchise. After elections, the leader of the majority party forms the government.' It is a precise answer, which the child is expected to remember. Wake up a 'well-educated' child at midnight and pose the question, pat comes the reply. We would feel good in that the child has said the correct answer.

But the new textbooks adopt a better route, even though it is longer. They first describe election campaigns and various arrangements necessary for conducting elections (like constituencies, parties, voter eligibility, and so on). This is followed by a narrative of how voting takes place, and the results across the state. Finally it shows who could have formed the government. Such a description draws in several ideas that were earlier excluded—like the idea that political parties are involved, and that people vote on different considerations. The new textbooks invite the children to identify what had happened in their state during the previous election (see Extract 4.3). We believe that this method is more useful to the child when she wants to understand what she reads in the newspapers—elections and government formation.

4.1 WHY ELECTIONS?

Do most leaders fulfil their election promises?

Assembly Election in Haryana

The time is after midnight. An expectant crowd sitting for the past five hours in a chowk of the town is waiting for its leader to come. The organisers assure and reassure the crowd that he would be here any moment. The crowd stands up whenever a passing vehicle comes that way. It arouses hopes that he has come.

The leader is Mr. Devi Lal, chief of the Haryana Sangharsh Samiti, who was to address a meeting in Karnal on Thursday night. The 76-year-old leader, is a very busy man these days. His day starts at 8 a.m. and ends after 11 p.m. ... he had already addressed nine election meetings since morning... been constantly addressing public meetings for the past 23 months and preparing for this election.

This newspaper report is about the State assembly election in Haryana in 1987. The State had been ruled by a Congress party led government since 1982. Chaudhary Devi Lal, then an opposition leader, led a movement called 'Nyaya Yudh' (Struggle for Justice) and formed a new party, Lok Dal. His party joined other opposition parties to form a front against the Congress in the elections. In the election campaign, Devi Lal said that if his party won the elections, his

government would waive the loans of farmers and small businessmen. He promised that this would be the first action of his government.

The people were unhappy with the existing government. They were also attracted by Devi Lal's promise. So, when elections were held, they voted overwhelmingly in favour of Lok Dal and its allies. Lok Dal and its partners won 76 out of 90 seats in the State Assembly. Lok Dal alone won 60 seats and thus had a clear majority in the Assembly. The Congress could win only 5 seats.

Once the election results were announced, the sitting Chief Minister resigned. The newly elected Members of Legislative Assembly (MLAs) of Lok Dal chose Devi Lal as their leader. The Governor invited Devi Lal to be the new Chief Minister. Three days after the election results were declared, he became the Chief Minister. As soon as he became the Chief Minister, his Government issued a Government Order waiving the outstanding loans of small farmers, agricultural labourers and small businessmen. His party ruled the State for four years. The next elections were held in 1991. But this time his party did not win popular support. The Congress won the election and formed the government.

Source: NCERT political science textbook, *Democratic Politics*, standard 9, p. 57.

121 **But why is the second (new) method better than the first?**

The old textbooks give the child knowledge (or information), but do not tell her how to use it. She may accurately recall what is there in the textbook about formation of government, but she may not be able to apply her knowledge to a concrete situation. After all, we want the child to understand the political process in the country. The detailed example in the new textbook provides a rich experience that enables the child to understand a situation. The new emphasis is not on merely providing information to the child, but on enabling him/her to use it as well.

Information recall can be one of the objectives of education, but it is not the only objective. Education should also help the child understand her own life and the world around. This is applicable to all school teaching, not just social science teaching.

Question 62

Question 62

Box 4.3

Tushar's Train Journey

Tushar was going from Delhi to Chennai for his cousin's wedding. They were travelling by train and he had managed to squeeze into the window seat, his nose glued to the glass pane. As he watched trees and houses fly past, his uncle tapped his shoulder and said: "Do you know that trains were first used about 150 years ago, and that people began using buses a few decades later?" Tushar wondered, when people couldn't travel quickly from one place to another, did they spend their entire lives wherever they were born? Not quite.

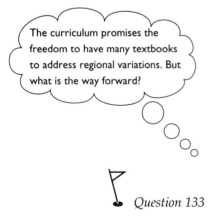

The curriculum promises the freedom to have many textbooks to address regional variations. But what is the way forward?

Question 133

Question 133

Textbooks and the Social Experience of Children

122 How can a textbook taught across a diverse country like India be sensitive to local, social experiences?

Yes, this is a weakness of 'national' textbooks. It is clear that the reference point in these textbooks is India (as a whole). The new textbooks try to minimize the weakness by using descriptions or narratives picked up from various regional settings, that is, children's experiences.

For example, in the history textbooks for standard 6, each chapter begins with a child's experience. Chapter 2 'On the Trail of the Earliest People' begins with a text panel (see Box 4.3).

That chapter then describes hunter-gatherers, their moving about, the rise of habitations, and so on. A few pages later, the chapter on Buddhism begins with a school trip (see Box 4.4).

In the political science textbooks, two children *Unni* and *Munni* pose questions on the margins of pages (see Extract 4.4). While a student in Kerala can relate to Unni ('the little one'), a student in Uttar Pradesh can relate to Munni.

Many feel that the problem of local experiences and meanings has not been properly addressed. The new geography textbooks deal with the country as a whole, without many regional touches. We need to incorporate the experiences of children from various regions in more ways.

Now I can see clearly! That is why they talk of Mandalisation of politics. Don't they?

Which institutions are at work in the running of your school? Would it be better if one person alone took all the decisions regarding management of your school?

Box 4.4————————

Anagha's School Trip

This was the first time Anagha was going on a school trip. They boarded the train from Pune (in Maharashtra) late at night, to go all the way to Varanasi (in Uttar Pradesh). Her mother, who came to see her off at the station, told the teacher: 'Do tell the children about the Buddha, and take them to see Sarnath as well.'

Box 4.5————————

This is the city where my cousin lives. I've been here only a few times. It is very big. Once, when I came here, my cousin took me around. We left the house early in the morning. As we turned the corner onto the main street we saw that it was already buzzing with activity. The vegetable vendor was busy arranging tomatoes, carrots and cucumbers in baskets at her stall...

123 There is very little that is common between the experiences of an urban child and a rural child, or between one living in Ladakh and another in Lakkidi. So how did you bring their experiences into the classroom?

For standard 6, there is a textbook titled *Social and Political Life*. The last chapter in it is on urban livelihoods. It is in the form of a narration by a rural (or small-town) child visiting a big city. It begins as in Box 4.5.

It uses a survey conducted in Ahmedabad to talk about people working on the streets. The chapter talks of street vendors, women in small business, factory workers, salesmen and marketing managers. Through the story of a cycle-rickshaw puller in Delhi who has come from Bihar (see Extract 4.5), and similar examples, the chapter draws out concepts like income disparities, working conditions, job security, and so on.

A similar presentation style is adopted in its preceding chapter too, which is on rural livelihoods. It describes a village in Tamil Nadu, through portraits of agricultural labourers and others.

The history textbook describes lives of people in forests and of nomadic pastoralists.

124 Interesting. But these are not the experiences of most children in classrooms where the textbooks are used.

A 'national' textbook, that is, one used across India, cannot incorporate the experiences of every child or all the experiences of any single child. The old history textbooks taught empires that did not extend to where I lived. But can I argue that those chapters and maps were useless? As a student, when I read the experience of another child in India, it was an opportunity for me to learn a different way of thinking about my own social experience. By using such examples as starting points for discussion, the teacher can widen the child's horizon to recognize differences in social experiences and in their light, evaluate one's own social experience. In fact, the new textbooks encourage this. The new history textbooks, for instance, ask the children to identify themselves with the experiences of people from various historical periods. Children are asked to write dialogues, narratives and pamphlets by using the information given in the textbooks.

Extract 4.5
Bringing Lives of Ordinary People into the Classroom

We bought a red rose and a yellow rose. On the pavement opposite we saw a person selling newspapers with a small crowd of people around him. Everyone wanted to read the news! Buses whizzed past and there were auto-rickshaws filled with school-children. Nearby, under a tree, a cobbler sat taking his tools and materials out of a small tin box. Next to him the roadside barber had begun his work: he already had a customer who wanted an early-morning shave!

A little way down the road, a woman was pushing along a cart with all kinds of plastic bottles, boxes, hairpins, clips etc. in it while

We came to a place where rickshaws were standing in a row waiting for customers. We decided to take one to the market, which was about two kilometres down the road.

Bachchu Manjhi – A Cycle-Rickshaw Puller

I come from a village in Bihar where I worked as a mason. My wife and three children live in the village. We don't own land. In the village I did not get masonry work regularly. The income that I earned was not sufficient for our family.

After I reached this city, I bought an old cycle rickshaw and paid for it in instalments. This was many years ago.

I come to the bus stop every morning and take the customers wherever they want to go. I work till 8.30 in the evening. I take rides of up to 6 kilometres in the surrounding area. Each customer gives me Rs. 5-10 per trip depending on the distance. When I'm ill I can't do this work, so on those days I don't earn anything.

I stay with my friends in a rented room. They work in a nearby factory. I earn between Rs. 80-100 every day, out of which I spend Rs. 50-60 on food and rent. The rest I save for my family. I visit my village two or three times a year to see my family. Though my family survives on the money I send, my wife also earns from agricultural work that she gets once in a while.

Source: NCERT social science textbook, *Social and Political Life-I*, standard 6, p. 78.

Box 4.6

Children Learn by Reading Local Experiences of Others, and Finding about Their Own

Where do you go when you are ill? Are there any problems that you face? Write a paragraph based on your experience.

Source: NCERT social science textbook *Social and Political Life-II*, standard 7, p. 24.

If you have seen crafts persons at work, describe in a short paragraph what they do. (Hint: how do they get the raw materials, what kind of equipment do they use, how do they work, what happens to the finished product).

Source: NCERT history textbook, *Our Pasts I*, standard 6, p. 98.

This 'problem of localization' in a national textbook has a flip side too, which we should not forget. At the age of 10–11 years (when the child is in standard 6), after five years of schooling, it is also necessary to broaden her vision beyond her immediate surroundings—to include other parts of India and the world.

125 **But doesn't this approach overload a textbook with details? For instance, a student in standard 9 or 10 is expected to know a lot of world events in political science textbooks.**

In the old system, children were expected to learn all the information in the textbooks. In that vein, when people look at a new textbook, they make the mistake of seeing it as merely a new storehouse of information. The purpose is often missed.

For example, by using the old textbooks, children were expected to remember the crop and vegetation patterns in various continents. That set of information was thought useful. The new, history textbook introduces vegetation patterns to explain how agriculture patterns changed in the United States and what effect they had on the landscape (see Extracts 4.6a, 4.6b and 4.6c). The purpose here is different—information is given not for the sake of giving information but to give the children a historical sense of the ways in which agriculture or the lives of farmers change.

Similarly, the descriptions of important events in world politics are not to teach about the events *per se* but to teach democracy—the topic of the textbook for standard 9. By giving such examples, we hope that children will be able to make sense of what happens in future—say a coup (like the recent one in Thailand) or the struggle for democracy (like in Nepal) or Emergency (like in Pakistan).

126 **We see social science being taught by teachers trained only in languages. Has the textbook taken care of such situations where a non-specialist is teaching the subject?**

Textbook writers, especially for standards 9 and 10, largely assume that the books will be taught by teachers trained in social sciences. The scenario you mention—language teachers teaching social sciences—is true in middle schools and some private high schools affiliated to the Central Board of Secondary Education (CBSE).

Extract 4.6a

The Issue is Important, not the Details

Fig.12 – The scythe was used for mowing grass before the mid-nineteenth.

Fig.13 – Breaking ploughs before the age of mechanisation.
(Courtesy: Fred Hultstrand History in Pictures Collection, NDIRS-NDSU, Fargo.)
You can see the twelve ploughs hitched to a team of horses.

Fig.14 – Seeding with drills and tractors. A highland farm in North Dakota, 1910. - (Courtesy: F.A. Pazandak Photgraphy Collection, NDIRS-NDSU, Fargo)
Here you can see three drills and packers unhitched from the tractor. The drills were about 10 to 12 feet long, each with about 20 disks drilling the soil for seeding. Packers followed behind the disks covering the seeds with soil. You can see the vast seeded field extending into the horizon.

Fig.15 – Breaking the ground on the Great Plains in North Dakota, 1910. (Courtesy: Fred Hultstrand History in Pictures Collection, NDIRS-NDSU, Fargo.)
You can see a Minneapolis steam tractor pulling a John Deere plough with metal shares that cut into the ground.
The plough could break the soil quickly and cut even strong grassroots effectively. Notice the deep furrows behind the machine and the unploughed land with grass on the left. Only big wheat farmers could afford these machines.

128

Source: NCERT history textbook, *India and the Contemporary World*, standard 9, p. 128.

cutting the crop. In 1831, Cyrus McCormick invented the first mechanical reaper which could cut in one day as much as five men could cut with cradles and 16 men with sickles. By the early twentieth century, most farmers were using combined harvesters to cut grain. With one of these machines, 500 acres of wheat could be harvested in two weeks.

For the big farmers of the Great Plains these machines had many attractions. The prices of wheat were high and the demand seemed limitless. The new machines allowed these big farmers to rapidly clear large tracts, break up the soil, remove the grass and prepare the ground for cultivation. The work could be done quickly and with a minimal number of hands. With power-driven machinery, four men could plough, seed and harvest 2,000 to 4,000 acres of wheat in a season.

2.4 What Happened to the Poor?

For the poorer farmers, machines brought misery. Many of them bought these machines, imagining that wheat prices would remain high and profits would flow in. If they had no money, the banks offered loans. Those who borrowed found it difficult to pay back their debts. Many of them deserted their farms and looked for jobs elsewhere.

But jobs were difficult to find. Mechanisation had reduced the need for labour. And the boom of the late nineteenth and early twentieth centuries seemed to have come to an end by the mid-1920s. After that, most farmers faced trouble. Production had expanded so rapidly during the war and post-war years that that there was a large surplus. Unsold stocks piled up, storehouses overflowed with grain, and vast amounts of corn and wheat were turned into animal feed. Wheat prices fell and export markets collapsed. This created the grounds for the Great Agrarian Depression of the 1930s that ruined wheat farmers everywhere.

2.5 Dust Bowl

The expansion of wheat agriculture in the Great Plains created other problems. In the 1930s, terrifying duststorms began to blow over the southern plains. Black blizzards rolled in, very often 7,000 to 8,000 feet high, rising like monstrous waves of muddy water. They came day after day, year after year, through the 1930s. As

Fig. 16 – Black blizzard in Western Kansas, 14 April 1935.

Peasants and Farmers

129

Source: NCERT history textbook, *India and the Contemporary World*, standard 9, p. 129.

Teaching Social Science in Schools • **78**

Fig.17 – Drouth Survivors. Painted by Alexander Hogue, (1936). Hogue dramatised the tragic scenes of death and destruction that he saw, in a series of paintings. Life Magazine *referred to Hogue as the artist of the dust bowl.*

the skies darkened, and the dust swept in, people were blinded and choked. Cattle were suffocated to death, their lungs caked with dust and mud. Sand buried fences, covered fields, and coated the surfaces of rivers till the fish died. Dead bodies of birds and animals were strewn all over the landscape. Tractors and machines that had ploughed the earth and harvested the wheat in the 1920s were now clogged with dust, damaged beyond repair.

What had gone wrong? Why these duststorms? In part they came because the early 1930s were years of persistent drought. The rains failed year after year, and temperatures soared. The wind blew with ferocious speed. But ordinary duststorms became black blizzards only because the entire landscape had been ploughed over, stripped of all grass that held it together. When wheat cultivation had expanded dramatically in the early nineteenth century, zealous farmers had recklessly uprooted all vegetation, and tractors had turned the soil over, and broken the sod into dust. The whole region had become a dust bowl. The American dream of a land of plenty had turned into a nightmare. The settlers had thought that they could conquer the entire landscape, turn all land over to growing crops that could yield profits. After the 1930s, they realized that they had to respect the ecological conditions of each region.

Source: NCERT history textbook, *India and the Contemporary World*, standard 9, p. 130.

A related problem exists in the majority of non-CBSE government and private schools. In Indian schools, a social science teacher may have studied (for B.A. or M.A.) only one or two subjects out of history, geography, economics, political science, sociology and psychology. Such specialization can hinder a teacher from preparing children for a common exam in social science. Even though there is commonality in the teaching methods of social science, the problem is serious. It needs to be addressed by teacher training institutions as part of their regular courses, or through refresher programmes (see Box 4.7).

127 Why not adopt an integrated social science curriculum?

While every one talks of integration, no one has been able to create model textbooks for social science. There has been very little movement in the direction of teaching social sciences as a single subject. Integration should not be merely binding a set of chapters from each subject into one book. There should be thematic integration. In the new textbooks, only a few themes have been discussed with cross-references to other subjects, and fall far short of what can be called integrated textbooks. Even 'alternative' social science textbooks (like Eklavya's) are oriented to meet the needs of subject specialization.

In India, we have not given sufficient thought to producing integrated textbooks. People seem to be waiting for a truly integrated curriculum before writing the textbooks for it.

128 How does an integrated curriculum benefit or affect the child?

With an integrated curriculum, we can reduce the quantity of information that the child has to learn. For this, social scientists should agree on what are the most important things that a child must know and what are the best ways for the child to learn. This has not been the starting point of either the new or earlier textbook projects. Only after a truly integrated textbook appears can we evaluate how a child responds to it.

A shared objective of social sciences is, in a broad sense, the understanding of society. People may understand society through various lenses—historical processes, economic and political systems, natural and geographical features—but it should be possible for each subject specialist to put forward what is most central in their discipline. As opposed to this

Box 4.7

Reach Out to Teachers, Parents, and Local Community Groups

Dialogue is, in fact, a key to the success of any endeavour that seeks to radically transform education. Unless a widespread process of dialogue is set in motion, the present textbooks run the risk of remaining yet another attempt at social engineering 'from the top'. Meaningful engagement of large numbers of ordinary schoolteachers will require concentrated efforts towards this end. Indeed, it will also be essential to reach out to parents and local community groups if the transformations envisaged are to become ground level reality.

Source: Deepti Priya Mehrotra, 'Texts and Contexts', *Seminar*, 569 January 2007.

ideal of integration, the present way is to engage the children from the concerns of each subject specialist.

Our present-day disciplines themselves emerged in the unique social and political context of the nineteenth century. While at one time it was the done thing to combine moral and political questions with economic inquiry, we have gradually seen a separation between political science on the one hand and economics on the other. Morality has become a disparaged term, meant only for a 'separate subject' called value education. The struggle to recreate an integrated social science is to transform the universities first, before we expect to see such an integration in schools. It is in the domain of methodology where many contemporary integrations are taking place. The NCERT textbooks' emphasis on methodology reflects this trend.

129 **Over the years, the tendency to 'catch them young' has been increasing. How has it affected the social science textbooks?**

On the one hand people talk of reducing the burden on the child; on the other, they think the solution to every problem is through schooling. Hence, you have the following tagged on to textbooks—disaster management (with geography); consumer education (with economics); environmental studies (with sciences); art, architecture and heritage (with history); human rights, (with political science) and so on (see Extract 4.7). Orders are passed to include a chapter on how to cross unmanned railway crossings or how to handle ragging in schools. The Supreme Court and the NGOs think of textbooks merely as an object to pass on an idea they think is important. These decisions are not always guided by any concern for the child, but the assumption that problems in our country can be resolved by making children aware of them.

130 **But isn't that a way of making education socially relevant?**

Some of these are social concerns and part of the main subjects taught in schools. But we need to resist the temptation that every social problem can be resolved through schooling. It only creates a jumble of superficial do's and don'ts. So many things get pushed in as one-liners, or a paragraph here and there, that when the child reads the final passage nothing sinks in. For complex issues, there should be proper treatment and discussion in a textbook. Only then can a textbook have an impact.

Extract 4.7
New Topics Keep Getting Added

CHAPTER 5
CONSUMER RIGHTS

The collage you see below contains some news clippings of consumer court verdicts. Why did the people go to the consumer court in these cases? These verdicts came about because some people persisted and struggled to get justice. In what ways were they denied justice? More importantly, what are the ways in which they can exercise their rights as consumers to get a fair deal from the sellers when they felt they had been denied a just treatment?

Source: NCERT economics textbook, *Understanding Economic Development*, standard 10, p. 73.

Also, when we write textbooks, it is important to keep in mind two key criteria: (*a*) what are the core ideas in a subject and (*b*) what level of complexity can a child grasp at a particular age. These themes then have to be developed in an appropriate sequence. Many themes are socially relevant, but one has to take hard decisions on how to spread them out over different textbooks across the 12 years of schooling. Otherwise we get dense textbooks which do not have any effect at all.

Teacher Autonomy

131 **A textbook binds the way a teacher performs in the classroom. It curbs teacher autonomy, does it not?**

Through a textbook, the state regulates the classroom practices of a teacher, one reason for which is to ensure quality and fix parameters for fair evaluation across the country. In India, good books for children are neither abundant nor accessible. If there were, say, good history books written with adolescents in mind, then a teacher could use these to build his own set of classroom practices. Based on their training at B.A. or M.A. levels, teachers could develop their own materials, but we do not see that happening yet. In this setting, if a teacher enjoys complete autonomy in developing the content relevant for his classroom, then wide differences (and discrepancies) may emerge across schools.

Also, when a school affiliates itself to boards like the CBSE or the Council for the Indian School Certificate Examinations (CISCE) the school and its teachers accept limits to their own autonomy.

While the basic dilemmas remain unresolved, the new textbooks do give more space to the teacher than previously. At the same time, they also demand that the teachers be up-to-date.

132 **For effectiveness, the new textbooks seem to highly depend on the ability of the teacher to interact with his class.**

Yes, especially when compared to the earlier textbooks. The new textbooks expect the teacher to be active and dynamic. The teacher, for instance, can decide how to use the material in the textbook—like narratives of people's lives or a child's experience—to build something.

But then, the content also directly addresses the child reader. While the teacher is expected to read and interpret the text, the child herself can probably understand the text on her own.

133 What are some of the problems faced by authors in preparing child-centric textbooks?

First, is the shortage of authors who are knowledgeable and skilled—people who know the advances in academic disciplines and are also capable of describing them well to children. The convention has been to get good scholars to write a textbook, so that its content will not be challenged. While such a textbook succeeds in confirming their scholarship, it may not connect with students because of the scholars' inaccessible and heavy style of writing. Even today, it is only the skills of a few people that have made some of these textbooks reader-friendly.

Second, is to visualize the child who will read the textbook. In the past, where alternative textbooks were made in various states, the audiences have been homogenous—students from the same region and those who speak the same language. But writing a textbook at the national level is a challenge. The child reader could be living anywhere—in the slums of Dharavi, or the flood plains of Bihar; in the trans-Himalayan region of Tawang, or on the sea coast of Orissa. Their language skills vary hugely, as do their social backgrounds and the exposure they have got. It is almost impossible to address them as a single unit.

Third, is to make the book attractive to the child. Photographs and images have to be selected with care—they must be thought-provoking to children. Here again, we feel the absence of skilled people who are both academically skilled and have the ability to visualize (or picturize) complex concepts for children. Some textbooks had good designers willing to creatively use their skills (see Extract 4.8).

Question 123

134 And what were the challenges faced by the authors in preparing textbooks that would satisfy adult critics?

Critics as a species are not uniform. They have different perspectives and play diverse roles.

Extract 4.8
One of the Best Illustrations

CHAPTER 9

A Shirt in
the Market

This chapter tells us the story
of a shirt ! It begins with the
production of cotton and ends
with the sale of the shirt. We
shall see that a chain of
markets links the producer of
cotton to the buyer of the
shirt in the supermarket.
Buying and selling takes place
at every step in the chain.
Does everyone benefit equally
from this? Or do some people
benefit more than others? We
shall find out.

Source: NCERT social science textbook, *Social and Political Life-I*, standard 7, p. 104.

One breed is that of adult researchers who unravel the underlying politics of the textbooks. Their studies read between the lines and typically highlight the upper-class bias, the urban bias, the male-centred world views, the biases against marginalized people (*dalit*s and tribals), and the state-centrism in any given textbook. Such readings result in strong criticisms of the textbooks, but often fail to put forward alternative material. Textbook writers have to stay on guard from this small (but vociferous) section of academic elites and ensure that the textbooks are not heavily biased. It is a challenge to write a textbook that does not merely reflect a statist world view.

Another breed consists of people waiting to see whether a textbook is driven by a single ideology. Those in the right will attack you for being towards the left, those in the left will blame you for not being sufficiently left, and those in the centre will anyway blast you left, right and centre! If you have attempted to balance the views, then they will say 'Oh, after all this is just a liberal opportunist.'

Similarly, each group wants a positive mention. One caste organization might declare that their caste's image has been tarnished and hence a particular reference should be removed. Later, it will reverse the demand and ask that the caste's role be mentioned in a positive light. It is a challenge to ensure that the sentiments of any section are not hurt.

Then there are the sceptics—people who claim that any text cannot be transacted because of inefficient schooling systems and facilities. They repeatedly refer to 'average' teachers and 'average' children, ask who will teach the improved textbooks, and tell us that teachers are not used to teaching the improved textbooks. But if that criticism is taken on board, then it is a chicken-and-egg situation, with no change possible. We need to start the change somewhere and we have started with textbooks.

135 Why is it so difficult to get reknowned scholars to write textbooks for children?

Textbooks for school children do not have the status of refereed journal articles or academic books. So, there is little incentive for good experts to be involved closely in preparing school textbooks. Some narrate their own experiences with bad textbooks (as student or parent), and sub-let the real work (of writing the textbooks) to educationists. For the new textbooks, many experts spent time and energy. But more time and serious discussion are required to produce great textbooks.

Pedagogic Approach

136 You say that this approach can be applied to teaching various social sciences. Please explain how you visualize history to be taught.

The new textbooks in history draw the attention of the students to the craft of the historian. This means learning to think for yourself in a rigorous manner and not relying upon others to tell you what is right or wrong. In history it means reading original sources and piecing together an accurate picture of the past to provide explanations for what happened. Note the commonality with the teaching of

NCF on How to Teach Social Sciences

History should be taught with the intent of enabling students better understand [how] their own world and their own identities came into being as shaped by a rich and varied past. History should now help them discover processes of change and continuity in their world, and to compare ways in which power and control were and are exercised.

Source: Excerpted from the National Curriculum Framework, 2005.

Box 4.9

NCF on How to Teach Social Sciences

In Political Science, the focus should be on discussing the philosophical foundations that underlie the value framework of the Indian Constitution, i.e. in-depth discussion of equality, liberty, justice, fraternity, secularism, dignity, plurality, and freedom from exploitation. As the discipline of Economics is being introduced to the child at this level, it is important that the topics should be discussed from the perspective of the people.

Source: Excerpted from the National Curriculum Framework, 2005.

science—through observations and experiments, teaching children how to reach their own conclusions. The focus is on the methods (of sciences or social sciences) to develop the thinking skills of students in these subjects. This is in contrast to providing the students with the final information and expecting them to merely memorize that.

137 How does the new textbook fit into the National Curriculum Framework?

The NCF 2005 comprises the state of art recommendations on how to conduct school education. Prepared by some of the best scholars in India, it is the product of generations of research and reflection on education. It is not infallible, but the NCF does put together the best informed guidelines available in India today. It bears excellent advice on how one should teach, what one should teach and how one should evaluate (see Boxes 4.8, 4.9 and 4.10).

Box 4.10

NCF on How to Teach Social Sciences

As pointed out by the Kothari Commission, the social science curriculum hitherto emphasised developmental issues. These are important but not sufficient for understanding the normative dimension, like issues of equality, justice, and dignity in society and polity. The role of individuals in contributing to this 'development' has often been overemphasised. An epistemological shift is suggested so as to accommodate the multiple ways of imagining the Indian nation. The national perspective needs to be balanced with reference to the local. At the same time, Indian History should not be taught in isolation, and there should be reference to developments in other parts of the world...

In order to make the process of learning participative, there is a need to shift from mere imparting of information to debate and discussion. This approach to learning will keep both the learner and the teacher alive to social realities...

Concepts should be clarified to students through the lived experiences of individuals and communities. It has often been observed that cultural, social and class differences generate their own biases, prejudices and attitudes in classroom contexts. The approach to teaching therefore needs to be open-ended. Teachers should discuss different dimensions of social reality in the class, and work towards creating increasing self-awareness amongst themselves and the learners.

Source: Excerpted from the National Curriculum Framework, 2005.

Some of the new textbooks are closer to the spirit of the NCF than others. They have been able to draw the students and teachers into greater involvement with the content. They have focused on central issues and principles rather than dull details. They have made much greater use of questions and exercises so as to enhance students' understanding. In these, the end-of-chapter exercises are not chore to be slogged through. Even where the textbooks do not live up in some respects to the NCF's standards (for example, in geography and class 9 economics), those who wrote them have tried hard. Yes, much more remains to be done.

International Politics and the Textbook

138 **There is a strong anti-US sentiment in the standard 9 textbook on democracy. Why is that?**

It would be wrong to assume that there is any sentiment against any country in the textbooks. To illustrate various themes, examples were drawn from across the world. These have included, along with the US, events and images from India, Britain, communist Poland, Pinochet's Chile, Saudi Arabia, former Yugoslavia, China and Ghana. Selection of examples was guided by the principle of choosing the best scenario which highlighted the ideas being discussed. The objective was not to portray any one country in a negative light, but to enable children to think about the complex political processes involved in democracy around the world.

Often, the descriptions were guided by two factors: how simple and straightforward the narrative was, and how best it would suit the situation or the concept being described. As happens in real life, some parts of the story depicted actions that supported democracy and some that opposed it. It was inevitable that in certain examples, the role of the US, the most powerful country in the world today, would come up. It is an unfortunate but widely recognized truth that in international affairs, the US has often allied itself with forces that were inimical to democracy. This is a strange paradox for a country that, within its own borders, has one of the more democratic political systems of the world and which claims democracy to be one of its defining national characteristics.

When we have to give examples of the saga of democracy across the world, it is inevitable that the questionable role of US foreign policy will occasionally be mentioned.

This is not a red slant against the US. Do also keep in mind that in the textbook, adjacent to the example of Chile (where, the Central Intelligence Agency helped to topple a democratically-elected government), is the example of Poland (where Solidarity led the struggle against the totalitarianism of the Soviet bloc). The hallmark of post-independence India was just this—we tried to stand straight and not lean against this or that world power.

Pedagogic Philosophy

139 Whose ideas were the sources of inspiration behind the current textbooks?

Over the last three decades, several advances have taken place in textbooks and classroom practices in small pockets across India. One can identify these not only in the works of NGOs like Digantar and Eklavya, but also in textbooks that came up in state initiatives like the Sarva Shiksha Abhiyan and the District Primary Education Programme in Kerala, and the Lok Jumbish in Rajasthan (see Extract 4.9). The SCERTs of Delhi and Chhattisgarh too evolved new models of textbooks and teaching practices. Such efforts, which showed alternatives to the traditional pattern of the NCERT textbooks, provided concrete and living examples to draw inspiration and ideas for rethinking and rebuilding the basics of textbook design in India.

Tagore and Gandhi were two Indian thinkers who influenced these changes. The approach of encouraging children to interact with the world and develop their understanding of it (rather than force them to listen to monologues) was given a rigorous grounding by philosophers and scholars like John Dewey, Jean Piaget, Lev Vygotsky and Jerome Bruner. The importance of an appreciation of the real world and its challenges was continually emphasized by Gandhi, and many others like Paulo Freire and Michael Apple, who saw education as part of humanity's struggle for emancipation (see Box 4.11). Vast literature is available now on these themes.

Box 4.11

Critical Pedagogy

Critical pedagogy provides an opportunity to reflect critically on issues in terms of their political, social, economic and moral aspects. It entails the acceptance of multiple views on social issues and a commitment to democratic forms of interaction. This is important in view of the multiple contexts in which our schools function. A critical framework helps children to see social issues from different perspectives and understand how such issues are connected to their lives. For instance, understanding of democracy as a way of life can be chartered through a path where children reflect on how they regard others (e.g., friends, neighbours, the opposite sex, elders, etc.), how they make choices (e.g., activities, play, friends, career, etc.), and how they cultivate the ability to make decisions. Likewise, issues related to human rights, caste, religion and gender can be critically reflected on by children in order to see how these issues are connected to their everyday experiences, and also how different forms of inequalities become compounded and are perpetuated. Critical pedagogy facilitates collective decision making through open discussion and by encouraging and recognising multiple views.

Source: Excerpted from the National Curriculum Framework, 2005.

Extract 4.9
Lok Jumbish Social Science Textbooks from Rajasthan

Source: Lok Jumbish textbook, *Samajik Adhyayan*, standard 6.

It was not as if people first sat and read everything and only then began to ask how better textbooks could be designed. People were already responding to the frustrations of the older approaches and were interacting with each other, reading the works of this scholar or that, looking at each other's efforts and simultaneously learning from all of these. There have been many people involved in the rethinking of school education who learnt not from reading scholarly books, but by their own collective engagement in changing education in India.

I 40 **This 'philosophy' of education you talk of was not discussed or debated, before being implemented. Is it not undemocratic? It looks like the capture of the NCERT by a small group of elites.**

Box 4.12

Popular Demands for Change

Hundreds of parents and teachers sent messages to NCERT in response to advertisements inviting public contributions for the National Curriculum Framework. One of these messages was from a Mumbai-based mother and teacher, Mrs Neeta Mohla. She wrote:

'...Our syllabus gets more massive and moves beyond the teaching capacity of the teachers, so they rush through the contents with tedious methodology.'

Source: Excerpted from the National Curriculum Framework, 2005.

The NCF was debated. Many people participated in it—not just academics or education professionals, but also parents, journalists and social activists (see Box 4.12). People from different walks of life joined this debate. So it is not fair to call it undemocratic. Also, the changes being adopted are based not merely on the opinions of people but draw their strength from research experiences of educationists, experiences of other countries and experiments in India.

Yes, at the most, a few hundred people have been central to this entire process. They may be the best minds in the business, but still the setting of the agendas of this effort continues to be dominated by a very small number of intellectuals in our country. It is less a question of party affiliation and more a problem of there being a very small number of good quality scholars and intellectuals in India to draw upon from. Until we are able to improve our higher education system and get a larger number of scholars willing to engage with questions of education (and not be diverted by other temptations), the problem will remain.

ABOUT THE AUTHORS

Alex M. George is an independent researcher in Eruvatty, Kerala, India. He was a member of the team led by Yogendra Yadav to develop the acclaimed political science textbooks for NCERT. He has over 10 years of experience in education, especially research in curriculum and developing of new material for schools. He has worked with Eklavya (Madhya Pradesh), Kanavu (Kerala), Students' Educational and Cultural Movement of Ladakh (SECMOL, Ladakh) and NCERT–CSDS (New Delhi). Apart from writing textbooks, Alex has written *Children's Perception of Sarkar: A Critique of Textbooks* (Eklavya, 2007).

Amman Madan is Assistant Professor at the Department of Humanities and Social Sciences, Indian Institute of Technology, Kanpur. He is a regular recipient of IITK's commendation letters for excellence in teaching based on feedback from students. He was a researcher with Eklavya (Madhya Pradesh) in 2002–03 and has held visiting positions at Tata Institute of Social Sciences (Mumbai), Homi Bhabha Centre for Science Education (Mumbai) and Jawaharlal Nehru University (New Delhi). His special areas of interest are sociology of education and the teaching of democracy in India. His articles have been published in English and Hindi periodicals like *Economic, Political Weekly, Contemporary Education Dialogue* and *Sandarbh*.